MY LIFE,
MY VALUES,
MY VOYAGE

Dear Joy and Bob.
Hope you enjoy my
story. You are wonderful
Friends. Thanks for all
the warmth you convey
to our Family!

Hershel

NOV 2016

MY LIFE,
MY VALUES,
MY VOYAGE

HERSCHEL KAHN

The author has tried to recreate events, locations, and conversations from his/her memories of them. In some instances, in order to maintain their anonymity, the author has changed the names of individuals and places. He/she may also have changed some identifying characteristics and details such as physical attributes, occupations, and places of residence.

ISBN: 978-0-9969648-0-7

Library of Congress Control Number: 2016949345

10 9 8 7 6 5 4 3 2   1 0 2 5 1 6

Printed in the United States of America

∞This paper meets the requirements of ANSI/NISO Z39.48-1992 (Permanence of Paper)

To my dear wife, Jody, my soul mate and love of my life,
I dedicate this collection of values.
How fortunate I am to have you as my lifelong tutor.

Life without values is a ship without a rudder.

Contents

FOREWORD

This book is a remarkable journey through the life of Herschel Kahn. The reader is not an observer, but an intimate participant in this wondrous work that inspires, touches, and transforms. Herschel, a man of incredible integrity and talent, teaches us how a proper, meaningful life is to be lived. He introduces us to his family, to his faith, to his soul. With humility, he shares the rich odyssey of his successful corporate career and passion for service. Herschel is the moral exemplar of the American Dream. I confess to feeling somewhat of a voyeur as I read this extraordinary book. I was pulled in, almost hypnotically, chapter after chapter. The honesty and intimacy shared is refreshing and enchanting. Though it is words and ink that fill the pages, it seems that the images created are done with loving detail by an artist and his brush. Complete a sentence, a paragraph, and one must pause in thought to absorb the gems tucked into this glorious narrative.

Nowhere in this work is there a whiff of arrogance or a breath of braggadocio, despite the soaring achievements of the author. To easily express the essence of this book is a challenge. It is a biography, yet it is not. It is a guide to righteous living, yet it is not. It is a strategy for fulfilling dreams, yet it is not. The sum of the pages does not adequately explain the totality of its work and its message. It is touching. It is faith. It is nostalgia. It is vision. It is hope. The serious reader cannot help being moved by the richness of Herschel's many years. Challenges were met and obstacles overcome in honorable fashion. We are witness to a happy truth: "Good guys can finish first."

Herschel's talent as a writer is his delightful, bountiful collection of anecdotes and memories that he shares freely and graciously. We also come to realize as we flip the pages that the book does not belong to the author, but to us, the readers. It is his gift to nourish and uplift us. In a world that extols shortcuts, sloth, and entitlements, this should be required reading. It is a celebration of diligence, loyalty, and values. I have known Herschel Kahn for many years, and there is no finer gentleman committed to living the noble, grand life.

—Rabbi Shalom Lewis, Congregation Etz Chaim

ACKNOWLEDGMENTS

I shall forever be indebted to my parents and grandparents, all the relatives, friends, coworkers, and teachers that instilled in me the values I have tried to live by. This effort to communicate what values I have learned from them is my way of demonstrating the respect and honor they deserve. To the entire staff of BookLogix: your professionalism brought my thoughts to life.

In the beginning

INTRODUCTION

In this book, I develop my belief that everyone begins his or her life's journey with a clean slate free of values. I maintain, for example, we are not born as honest, courageous, persevering, ethical, or caring individuals. As we travel the road called life, we gain the education, experience, and knowledge that become the foundation of our personal value infrastructure. Integral to this development phase of our values are the people from whom we have interacted with along our journey. These include but are not limited to grandparents, parents, siblings, relatives, friends, teachers, clergy, managers, neighbors, coworkers, or even those with whom we have no personal contact but merely observe from afar.

After "walking the walk" for over eighty years, I have memorialized in this work those values which I view as beacons of light that have guided me in living a most interesting, fulfilling, and meaningful life. I bring realism to how I acquired these values by sharing personal experiences demonstrating my interaction with people having significant impact in my life. I have melded some humor together with the earnest principles I wish to convey. Of particular note is the dedication to my wife Jody, my parents, and maternal grandfather.

The book clearly will motivate the reader to analyze their personal set of values. It is written in a warm, friendly, interesting, and meaningful style.

Assisting Others

Providing assistance to someone in need
Is an opportunity we should heed

As the years go by, there comes a day when one may ask him or herself, "Why am I here?"

Other questions are soon to follow. Have I made this a better place? Have I made a difference in someone's life? What have I accomplished that will serve as positive examples for others?

I truly believe we are here for a purpose. As we journey through life, opportunities to assist others become available to us. Responding to those opportunities in a positive way may be one purpose for our very being.

As a child, I witnessed numerous examples of family members reaching out to others to offer help. My dad would provide some basic furnishings to newly arrived immigrant families. He assisted other family members and successfully brought cousins that survived the Holocaust to the United States. He provided furniture to families on a "pay what you can whenever you can" basis. My mom volunteered her time to various organizations. My maternal grandfather somehow always had a few dollars available to help others. It wasn't until later in life that I realized the example they set and the value they were teaching.

As an adult, many situations to assist others have become available to me. To my great fortune, my loving wife Jody shares my view regarding assisting others. She even takes it to a higher level. Without her support, some things that have been accomplished would not have been possible.

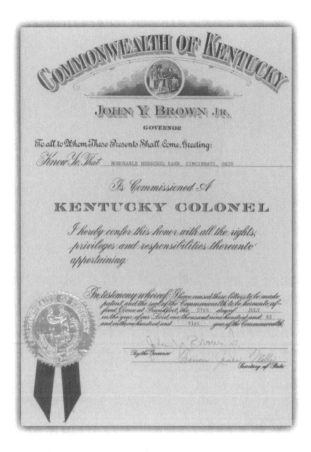

During my career with IBM, the company maintained a strong presence in the state of Kentucky. The relationship between our company and the state government was excellent. At one point in 1982 the governor of Kentucky requested some human resource advice from IBM. At that time my office was in Cincinnati which was in close proximity to an office the governor maintained in Lexington. I was asked to work with the governor to respond to his request. Prior to being elected to the office of governor he had a long and successful career in the private sector. His request was to determine the feasibility of implementing some private-sector human resource initiatives into a public-sector environment.

It was a challenging assignment and required numerous visits and meetings. The end result was successful. As a token of his appreciation the governor awarded me the honorary title of "Kentucky Colonel." While it has minimal significance outside the Commonwealth of Kentucky, it was a nice gesture on his part.

I thoroughly enjoyed the experience. By providing assistance the end result not only pleased the person requesting my help, it proved to be of help in the event I was ever cited for a Kentucky motor vehicle violation. Fortunately, the need never arose, but I treasure the document and the story about it.

We all have opportunities to help others in our daily lives. Many of these situations reflect common courtesy and how we were raised. Holding a door for someone, helping an elderly person cross the street, or writing a check to a charity clearly are such examples. When I speak of assisting others, my focus is on events that have a long-lasting, lifetime impact. While I have had a number of situations in my professional career to be of assistance to others, I viewed them as obligations. There are three situations, however, that I encountered which allowed me to apply the values learned by assisting others. The assistance provided had lifetime significance.

SITUATION 1

While in the military during 1957–1958, I was assigned to an installation located in Rochefort, France. I was a quartermaster officer and one of my responsibilities was the post commissary. A young French lady was assigned to the office staff as a requisition clerk. She was an excellent employee and she always had a most positive attitude. She was a widow with one very small child.

When my assignment in France was completed, I was discharged from active duty. Jody and I returned to Chicago to civilian life. Shortly after settling into our new surroundings, I received a letter from the French woman advising me that she had met a career soldier, fallen in love, and decided to marry. Unfortunately, the soldier had completed his assignment in France and was now in the United States. The lady needed a sponsor to arrange for her to come to the US. Her request was for me to be her sponsor. Her fiancé was ineligible to be her sponsor. At that point in time, a sponsor had to agree to assume financial responsibility for the individual for ten years. This was to ensure that, if difficulties arose, the person would not become a financial liability to the US government.

While our resources were quite limited, we decided to assist her. She arrived in Chicago and was met by her fiancé. We arranged for them to be married by a judge in City Hall, took them to a Chinese restaurant for dinner, loaned them fifty dollars for gasoline, and wished them well as they departed for their new military assignment in Florida. We believed we did the right thing, never thought we would see the return of the fifty dollars, and thought we would probably not hear from them again. How wrong we were. Each month for ten months, she sent us five dollars with a note of how well things were going and how happy they were. The years passed, her husband retired, and they settled in Williamsburg, Virginia. She became a US citizen and worked as a seamstress sewing colonial uniforms for the museum in Williamsburg. We maintained close contact with her and her family over all the years. This "young" lady is now in her nineties, living with her "little" girl and her extended family. Her husband is now deceased. The assistance we provided so many years ago has been a source of fulfillment to us. It truly was a life-changing experience for the lady and one that we shall always cherish.

SITUATION 2

This event occurred in 1995. I had been retired from IBM for three years and decided that perhaps I could utilize my corporate experience to assist other business entities. I enrolled as a volunteer for the International Executive Service Corps (IESC). This is an organization that provides professionals with expertise in various disciplines to foreign companies. My enthusiasm was tested when I was offered an assignment in St. Petersburg, Russia, in January of that year.

When Jody heard St. Petersburg, she immediately thought of Florida and was shocked when she learned it was a different St. Petersburg. I made five requests of the organization:

1. My wife would need to accompany me.
2. I needed a driver since I could not read Russian.
3. I requested an interpreter since I did not speak Russian.

4. I would like an apartment with heat and hot water.
5. I wanted at least four hours per day with the owner of the enterprise so that I could accomplish something.

In return, my service would be completely voluntary. All was agreed to by the IESC organization. I then asked Jody if she would go with me on this adventure.

She replied, "You are asking me to leave Atlanta and go to Russia in the middle of winter?" However, true to form, and ever the adventurer, she said, "If that is something you want to do, I'm with you!" And off we went.

The assignment was assisting a young Russian entrepreneur and his wife, who founded a startup enterprise that distributed desktop computers. While on vacation in Finland, he discovered that he could purchase a computer and sell it upon his return to Russia for a small profit. Hence, the light of capitalism was ignited, and he decided that if he bought more and sold more, he would improve his financial position. The learning curve for my friend was quite steep, but he was most eager to implement Western business practices. We had some incredible learning experiences, many laughs, and some not-so-funny experiences.

While the overwhelming experiences with the Russian adventure were most positive, there were several that I could have lived without. The first occurred during the very first week we lived in St. Petersburg. On a pleasant Saturday afternoon, Jody and I decided to take a walk down one of the main streets of this very beautiful city. Being quite naïve, I had my video camera in plain view on the outside of my jacket. All was going well until I was suddenly surrounded by a group of young boys who jumped on me, forcing me to the ground, whereupon they tried to take the video camera. Together, with assistance from some passing Good Samaritans, we were able to fend them off. I was able to retain the camera, although my glasses were damaged. That experience taught me very quickly to keep all valuables out of sight.

International Executive
Service Corporation plate

While in St. Petersburg, our two daughters, Michele and Hannah, decided to visit their parents to see how we were faring. They arrived in March, which was also Hannah's birthday. As a surprise, we decided to travel to Moscow for some sightseeing. As an added bonus, we purchased tickets to a performance of the Bolshoi Ballet, the premier ballet company in Russia. We were in our seats with great anticipation of a most entertaining evening. The performance was delayed past the scheduled opening time, and the audience grew somewhat restless. After some further delay, a spokesman for the ballet appeared on stage and gave a short speech in Russian. At that point, the spectators began booing and started to exit the venue. When we asked if there was a problem, we were informed the ballet company was staging a strike, and there would be no performance. Furthermore, there would be no refund of admission fees. The Bolshoi Ballet Company was founded in 1825, and this was a first. It was a very disappointing experience, but at least we did get to see the beautiful facility.

Another not-so-fun experience occurred one day when the water in our apartment building was shut off. After finding someone that could explain what happened, I learned "the problema" was that the main water main for the structure had broken. I then asked what I believed to be a reasonable question: "How long until it will be repaired?"

The answer? "Whenever they get to it." Finally, after three days, the repairs were made. The crew assigned to the project was in no hurry, the entire project was done without any mechanical equipment, and there did not appear to be any urgency on the part of anyone involved. At that time, there was a joke circulating about an individual that purchased a new automobile and asked the salesperson, "When may I expect delivery?"

"Exactly six months from today," the salesperson replied.

The client then asked, "In the morning or afternoon?"

"What difference does it make?" the dealer asked. "We are talking about six months from now."

"Because the plumber is coming in the morning," the client answered.

At that point in time there were five employees, working in somewhat cramped quarters and generating a very modest income. My friend was most receptive to my counsel and help, and we worked very well together.

Jody and I had a great time enjoying all the culture St. Petersburg offered. We weathered the harsh winter, and enjoyed our daughters' visit. I felt very good about providing assistance to my Russian friend. He implemented many suggestions and was most appreciative of my help. Over the years, I maintained contact with both him and his wife. It was gratifying to see how they were prospering and growing their business.

Seventeen years passed, and in 2012, Jody thought it would be a good idea to visit Russia in the summer and sample the country in a different season. We told our Russian friends of our planned visit. They were delighted and insisted on hosting us during our visit to St. Petersburg.

It was wonderful to see them again. The business had grown to over one thousand employees, and what was once a modest revenue stream had evolved into a very significant asset.

Upon reflection, the assistance I was able to provide made a difference not only in the life of my friend, but I believe it also made a difference in the lives of the many people that were involved in the business venture.

Value Learned: There are good days, and there are bad days. Hopefully, there are more good than bad. If things are not going well, remember tomorrow is a new day—greet it with positive thoughts.

SITUATION 3

There are times when you seek an opportunity to be of assistance. There also are times when someone seeks your assistance. It is the latter event that is most difficult, since it involves a decision process to determine two things. First, do you have the experience and knowledge to be of help? Secondly, do you have the will, time, and motivation to be of help? The situation I am about to describe presented a most difficult decision. I had neither the experience, knowledge, nor expertise to help a friend who was reaching out to me.

Jody and I had traveled from Atlanta to Cincinnati for a social event. It was a Saturday evening, and we were asleep when the phone rang. It was a friend of mine calling from Atlanta. This individual was the lead executive of a rather large company.

The conversation began with my friend wanting to say goodbye to me. I asked him what he meant by that comment. He replied that his business was failing and he believed it was due to his inability to manage it properly. He thought it best if he were to take his own life as accepting full responsibility for the unfortunate event. Having this situation thrust upon me without any preparation, in the middle of the night, in a foggy state of mind, and no professional expertise was a challenge to say the least.

I wanted to help but had no idea what to do. The only thing I could think of was to convince the individual to hold his thoughts until I could return home the following evening to speak to him face to face. After what seemed forever, he agreed to wait and talk with me when I returned. There was no further return to sleep for me that night.

The next day I met with him. All I could think of was the simplest and basic approach to solving a problem. We took out a sheet of paper and we jointly wrote down alternatives to try before implementing his choice. I remember suggesting, "Let's try all these other choices first. If they fail, you can always go with your plan. However, should you choose your solution first, we will never be able to see if one of the other ideas would have succeeded." He did agree and his demise was avoided.

The problems facing my friend consisted of inadequate cash flow, declining sales, and a corporate executive team that was both unyielding and unwilling to render assistance. I suggested some measures for him to consider. These included factoring his accounts receivable, reducing nonessential staff, and implementing an incentive program to stimulate sales. He did not embrace these suggestions, as he was not confident they would bring the necessary results. From a cultural perspective, failure was tantamount to a capital crime. At that point, I had a lengthy discussion to convince my friend that there are far worse things in life than a failing business venture. I reasoned with him that he had a family to care about, years ahead of him to see his children mature, raise families, and enjoy what life has to offer. The solution I proposed was to resign his position, consider it a lesson of life, go on to another venture, and look ahead rather than back. He had a lifelong interest in music and teaching young people to play various instruments. He could do something he enjoyed, eliminate the pressure and stress of running a business, and enjoy life while fulfilling his passion for music. He accepted my counsel and today is content, free of stress, happy, enjoying his family, and looking forward to each day.

In retrospect, what I did was nothing more than applying logic to solve a perplexing problem. I tried to start with the end result I planned to achieve. In that case, it was to persuade my friend to not self-destruct. While recognizing the significance of the problem for my friend, I tried to convince him that there is more to life than being successful at one endeavor.

I never will forget that experience. It truly was a life-changing event for someone. My assistance was at best a most juvenile approach to helping a friend. The value learned was that assistance takes many different forms. It doesn't have to be sophisticated—just simple and sincere.

Value Learned: There are times when you must take a step back to eventually take two steps forward.

DAD'S GOLDEN RULE

Contrary to all the books, articles, videos, and lectures promoting negotiating skills, Dad simply did not believe in that art. He had a rather unique style concerning the purchase or sale of any item. It made no difference if it was real estate, an automobile, furniture, jewelry, or appliances.

In his mind, he would establish what he thought to be a fair price. The number would allow a fair profit to the seller as well as a reasonable value for the buyer. The operative words being what **"he thought was fair."**

I observed how he would deal with customers in a very friendly manner while remaining firm to a stated price. I also saw that when he purchased something, he never attempted to negotiate. There came a day when I asked him why he did not negotiate. His answer was not only interesting but quite amusing. He asked if I believed in the Golden Rule. I answered yes but asked what that had to do with my question.

He replied, "Herschel, I have my own 'Golden Rule.'" He continued with some advice. "Before you purchase something, do your homework and determine what is a fair price by doing some comparative shopping, reading, or asking questions. If you follow that routine, there really is no reason to spend time and effort to achieve minimal gain. The same protocol should be followed when selling something." He concluded his lecture with, "I call that my Golden Rule. What that means is 'he who has the gold makes the rule.'"

Value Learned: My takeaway from this lecture is when purchasing or selling an item, do your homework, be fair to both parties, and never underestimate the leverage of your financial position.

BUSINESS

Business is more than dollars and cents
Key to success is using common sense

Many of my family members were very entrepreneurial. They founded and ran their small ventures and all managed to be successful. Their businesses were a source of great pride that tested their resourcefulness and provided a comfortable livelihood. When I was a youngster, they became my role models. I decided that I, too, would pursue a business career.

After graduating from high school, I knew I needed to get a college education if I wanted to achieve my long-term goals. My dad asked me what I planned to study at the university. I quickly answered, "Business."

He looked at me, and without hesitation said, "That has to be one of the dumbest decisions you could ever make." I asked why he felt that way and his response was quite clear. "Son, people go to college to learn medicine, law, engineering. Not business." I understood the source of his comments because the business contemporaries of his day had not gone to college. He himself immigrated to the United States in his late teens. He never had the opportunity to receive any formal education and personified the self-made individuals of his era.

The lesson continued as he described his position more fully. He clearly knew what would be taught at the university level. He talked about economics, accounting, business law, finance, and even touched on a course in statistics. This was impressive given that he never had any exposure to academics.

13

S. KAHN	B. KAHN
Hy. 8188	Hy. 2827

KAHN BROTHERS

COMPLETE HOUSEHOLD FURNISHINGS

Telephone Hyland 6036

813 and 815 West Broadway   MINNEAPOLIS, MINN.

Kahn Brothers business card

After his initial reaction to my choice of curriculum, he asked me to come into his office. He had a very old wooden desk. He placed a stack of unpaid invoices on the desk. Next to the invoices he placed his company checkbook.

The lesson then began. "Son, I take one invoice from this stack and write a check in payment. I continue the process until I see one of two things. If the invoices have been paid and I can see the wooden top of my desk and a positive balance remains in the checkbook, I am successful. However, if the balance in the checkbook has reached zero and unpaid invoices remain, I have failed. Keep it simple, my boy!"

Dad concluded the lesson by restating his original advice. "I just taught you something that has saved you four years of your time and many dollars. Study something that is more challenging than just using common sense."

I did follow my game plan and earned a BBA degree, and some years later, an MBA. I never regretted my decision. However, I never forgot the message my dad was trying to convey. Many years have passed since that lesson in his office, and I often think back to that experience. During my professional career—whether at IBM, volunteering in academia, consulting, or as a board member of various companies—I have sat through countless financial presentations. I smile to myself as the presenter articulates multiple financial metrics. The list is endless. For example:

- EBITA (Earnings Before Interest, Taxes, and Amortization)
- EBITDA (Earnings Before Interest, Taxes, Depreciation, and Amortization)
- Debt to Equity Ratio
- Time Value of Money
- Marginal Cost
- Passive Income
- Schedule of Depreciation
- Inventory Turn
- Earnings per Share

The list goes on and on. I think back to what my dad described with his invoice-and-checkbook example and smile as my eyes drift down to the bottom line of the last chart that reads "NET PROFIT" or "LOSS."

Clearly, there is no comparison involving a sole proprietorship furniture store circa 1930s to the megacorporations and organizations of today. Regulations, controls, accounting practices, governance requirements, and due diligence compliance are but a few examples of protective procedures that have been put in place. However, when assessing the success of a business, it still comes down to the number on the bottom line regardless of how many pages it takes to get there. "Keep it simple, my boy!"

The value of what my dad learned, and what he was trying to impart to me, is that the primary objective of a business is to make a profit. A good idea, good service, good customer relations, hiring people, a fine product, and community relations all depend on a business being profitable. None of these lofty goals and objectives would be possible if the enterprise was not profitable. He drew a sharp distinction between a profitable and a charitable organization. He held in high regard his customers, the service he provided, fair pricing, and ethical behavior. He clearly understood that without retaining customers as well as attracting new customers, a business could not survive.

Value Learned: Never underestimate the value of goodwill, even though it does not appear as a line item on a balance sheet.

CARING

Showing you care is a source of comfort
It will be warmly received and well worth the effort

Understanding and appreciating that every person we interact with has his or her own personal universe is an acquired skill. The ability to demonstrate that we care about them as individuals is not only appreciated by the recipient but can also be very self-fulfilling. As a youngster, I recall my mother exchanging greetings with whomever she came in contact with. Whether it was the milkman, mailman, or the grocery-store owner, she would take a few minutes and inquire about how their day was going. At the time, I didn't understand her reasoning for engaging in small talk. I looked upon it as a waste of time. Sometimes, the conversations became two-way, and she would provide updates about our family. It was much later in life that I realized in her own way, my mother, by showing interest in people, made them feel significant beyond just providing services.

As I grew older, my mother continued to stress the importance of caring for others. She taught me to hold the door for elders, to offer to assist people with carrying their groceries, and to pick up a dropped article for someone. She always reminded me that someday I would be old and someone would offer help. I laughed. I could not imagine being old.

The greatest teacher of caring is my dear wife, Jody. If there ever is a higher education degree awarded for caring, she will be *magna cum laude*. Over our many years together, we have met untold numbers of people. It has been a privilege and one of life's great treasures to have met so many people. We have visited over eighty-five countries, been to all fifty states, lived in Minnesota, Indiana, Illinois, Virginia, Connecticut (twice), Ohio, France, Russia, and currently Georgia, and worked thirty-three years for one company. With all that exposure, the numbers of contacts grew exponentially. It is one thing to meet someone at a point in time. It is quite different to maintain an ongoing relationship with people over many years. Jody is absolutely fantastic at keeping in touch with people we have met years ago. She maintains contact, and whenever we travel near someone we have met previously, she makes every effort to contact them. As the years have passed, the numbers continue to grow—as children of individuals we met have become adults, they too are added to the inventory, many of whom have made their way into her address book. She maintains contact with a significant number and maintains communication through phone, cards, and an annual letter. As the years passed, second-generation members have been added to this database.

One of Jody's hobbies is quilting. As the second generation of friends and relatives becomes parents, Jody handcrafts a baby quilt to commemorate the event. Each quilt is personalized and is truly a work of art. This activity takes caring to a new level. Jody will go to great lengths to customize the baby quilt. She will ask questions of the parents such as the baby's name, colleges attended by the parents, a pet's name, a favorite sports team, hobbies (for example if the parents like golf or tennis, she will include a golf or tennis symbol), or the parents' professions (doctor, lawyer, computer technology, etc.). The result is a custom quilt that has a lasting meaning due to the personalized effort that captured things of importance to the family.

I have learned that caring for others has one primary and fundamental requirement: sincerity. If we care about someone and decide to express our feelings, it must be offered in the spirit of sincerity.

My mother, Bessie Kahn

Examples of small things that mean a great deal to others:

- Remembering significant dates such as birthdays and anniversaries
- Calling to inquire recovery status from an illness
- Offering assistance with a stressful situation
- Visiting someone in a hospital or assisted living facility
- Sending condolence letters
- Volunteering to assist a nonprofit organization
- Calling a friend you have not been in recent contact with to say hello

19

- Taking someone shopping who has no means of transportation
- Providing professional assistance *gratis*
- Hosting a social event to bring friends together

There are times when we are preoccupied with our own goals and issues. We are unwilling or unable to think about others. It is at times like these when it becomes therapeutic to take a few moments and realize how meaningful it would be if someone reached out to us with some form of encouragement. This introspection will serve us well when we have an opportunity to care about someone else. The satisfaction one realizes when someone says thanks for remembering or caring far surpasses any expectation of something in return.

Upon reflection of my own life, I feel very fortunate and blessed that I have had the opportunity and ability to care about others. It is a source of great pride that some individuals I assisted in my career with IBM achieved success. In a consultant capacity, it has been intellectually rewarding to experience the satisfaction gained from caring about people and organizations. On a personal level, both Jody and I have imparted to our children the value of learning to care about others and the return on the investment they will enjoy.

Caring demonstrates a genuine interest in others. The recipient appreciates the fact that someone is interested in them personally. It brings comfort to the provider in that it gives a sense of purpose that is both fulfilling and meaningful.

Value Learned: Our purpose in life is more than to amass things for ourselves. Thinking of others brings comfort and pleasure that cannot be purchased.

CHARITY

Responding to charity is a selfless act
It makes one feel good, that is a fact

My earliest introduction to charity occurred when I was about five or six years old. On a kitchen counter close to the back door, my mother had a small blue-and-white metal container for collecting coins. Printed on the front were the words "Jewish National Fund." It was very typical of my parents to drop some coins into the box when they entered our home. I remember asking my mom why they did this. She explained the money was collected and sent to a place called Palestine to plant trees. She told me people who have a beautiful yard should help other people who are not fortunate enough to plant trees. It was only as an adult that I made the effort to learn more about this organization. The Jewish National Fund was founded in 1901 with the purpose of purchasing and developing land in Ottoman Palestine, which subsequently became Israel. The JNF organization claims to have planted over 240 million trees in Israel. It also has built dams, reservoirs, and parks. Charitable contributions have made this possible. As I grew older and earned a weekly allowance, the lesson of charity continued, and I was encouraged to donate some part of my allowance to help others.

The charitable theme in our home was reinforced with conversations focused on helping people in need. Whether it was the Red Cross, Cancer Fund, Heart Fund, or numerous other charities, they all received some attention.

My grandfather, Morris Goldman

One example of charitable giving was something my grandfather did that will forever remain etched in my memory. My grandfather was a dedicated family person but not someone of wealth. He worked exceedingly long hours to provide for his family. Late in life, he was fortunate to realize some financial gain resulting from the sale of the land upon which his business was located. He was then in a position that allowed him to retire and enjoy his remaining years. One of his favorite pastimes was to read newspapers from cities other than Minneapolis. One day, he came upon a story of a family in Nebraska that lost their home and belongings as a result of a fire. He called my mom late one evening and asked her to send some money to help the family. She asked him some basic questions such as name, address, amount to send, and what message he would like to provide.

"You figure it out—just get it done." The lesson he was trying to teach in his own way was that it is not necessary to know specific details. If you recognize the need and have the resources, it is incumbent upon you to reach out and help someone in need.

Fortunately, my lovely bride Jody was raised in an environment with the same charitable values as my family. She maintains her own income stream and selects various organizations that she deems worthy of charitable contributions. If animals could talk or write letters, she would be inundated with their thank you notes. Veteran and environmental organizations also receive their share of her recognition. Our mail carrier has job security and must smile every day with the volume of solicitations. While generosity is a key component of her personality, she also is very much aware that there are some unscrupulous individuals who will take advantage of an individual's generosity. For that reason, she does her due diligence.

Writing a check, dropping some coins into a kettle during the holidays, buying a meal for someone, or contributing in any other way to an individual or an organization are all examples of giving. Charity is not limited to monetary contributions. One of our most precious assets is time. To donate some of our time to assist others is a personal commitment that is even more lasting than financial help.

Sharing, caring, and contributing are all exemplary virtues. The feeling of satisfaction one experiences after helping someone is exceptional. The act of helping someone in need using whatever resource we have goes a long way in answering the question, why are we here?

Charity allows a person to share something he or she has with others that are less fortunate. It is not limited to monetary assets, but can include perishable and nonperishable items as well as intellectual property and assistance. If someone is fortunate enough to be able to render assistance to someone in need, the result is a feeling of satisfaction that you have helped someone in some way. The act may very well perpetuate itself when the person you have helped has an opportunity to help someone else. To the contrary, in the event a person elects not to be charitable, he or she could very well be haunted by other questions:

"Whatever became of the person or organization in need?"

"I wonder if I could have made a difference and changed the eventual outcome?"

Value Learned: Sharing something we have with someone in need is beneficial to both.

COMPASSION

Compassion for others is wonderful to do
Tomorrow it may be shown to you

"We are not alone in this world; we should look at others." Those words were spoken on more than one occasion by my parents. Many times around the kitchen table, a story about some unfortunate situation was discussed. For example: Immediately after World War II, my father became aware that some relatives had survived the Holocaust and were seeking asylum in the United States. My dad and his cousins discussed how they could provide assistance in bringing the family to America. They were successful—the family did arrive and went on to live out their lives in comfort and safety. Another example pertains to a situation that involved my mother's sister, who was diagnosed with a terminal illness. The family came together to determine who would be responsible for the care of the children upon her death. This was done not only for the benefit of the children, but was also an act of compassion for their father.

The value of compassion manifested itself in my adult life:

Upon our return from our military service in France, we found an apartment and settled in Chicago. There was a friend of ours who taught school with Jody in France. She also returned about the same time and settled in Chicago. The woman had very limited funds and could not afford an apartment. We offered to help, and she lived with us until she found a position and could afford her own apartment.

During my career with IBM, I was fortunate to be in positions where I could influence some hiring decisions. There were occasions that I was able to assist friends who were unemployed in securing employment with IBM. It was mutually beneficial as they went on to have successful careers of their own.

Compassion is not limited to human interaction. Our family has great affection for animals. Over the many years of our marriage, there have been at least a dozen stray and abandoned dogs and cats that have come to our door for a "handout." Each one in turn was taken in as a family member and lived a changed life. We joke that when they arrived at our home they "won the lottery" and had no further worries about their future welfare.

One particular experience brought the message home to me. Part of the revenue from my dad's furniture business was derived from installment payments. He never charged interest but was content to accept whatever the client could pay until the balance was paid in full—the operative word being "content."

My dad would typically make house calls on Sundays when people were back from church and usually at home. He would always invite me to accompany him. In my mind, he was doing this to either teach me his business or he was just proud to show off his young son. I never understood until much later what his true motive was. He made sure I was wearing nice clothes and looked "presentable."

The one memory that stands out and was a lifetime experience occurred one Sunday when I was about eleven years old. We set off to make our rounds like any other Sunday. However, on this particular day, we visited a small family in their apartment and something different happened. In those days, visiting was conducted around the dining room table. Family rooms were quite uncommon and TV was nonexistent, so the dining room or kitchen table served as the focal point for meetings. People could gather around the table. There most likely was a bowl of fruit in the center of the table and conversations would take place. It was a comfortable and friendly setting.

After a pleasant conversation that lasted about one hour, my dad suggested that it was time for us to depart and let the family enjoy the rest of their day. We left, and my dad headed for his next call. En route, I decided to ask my dad a question: "Dad, we visited with the last family for about an hour. I thought our purpose in stopping at their apartment was to collect some money." My dad smiled and said that he would explain the situation to me.

He began our conversation with some questions, the first being, "Do you recall where we met?" I replied, "In the dining room at the dining room table."

Next question: "Do you recall what was on the table?"

I answered again, "A large fruit bowl."

Next question: "What was in the fruit bowl?"

My answer, "There was nothing in the bowl." He complimented me for being observant, and the lesson began.

He told me that I was correct about my observations as well as the purpose of our visit. He then pointed out that since the bowl was empty, it was obvious the family at that point in time did not have the money to fill the bowl with fruit. Since they didn't have the funds to buy fruit, they certainly did not have the funds to pay any portion of their account. They knew one of the reasons for his visit. They also knew exactly the balance they owed. To ask for money served no purpose and it would only have embarrassed the family. When we visited them again, their situation may have improved, and they would be able to pay. We were fortunate that we had the funds to have fruit in our bowl. Not everyone was in that position.

Money is important, but you must always be able to understand that other things are even more important. You must recognize and understand that some people are less fortunate than we are. While money is important, it should not become our primary objective. Recognizing that some amount of money is necessary to maintain a comfortable lifestyle, the quest for it should not be allowed to control your life. Other, more enduring goals will ultimately bring greater satisfaction. Examples include, but are not limited to:

- Self-Fulfillment—When you reflect on your life, a question to ask is: have I accomplished all I set out to do?

- Self-Actualization—Did I utilize to the best of my ability my talents, skills, and intellectual capacity?
- Nonfinancial Accomplishments—Have I made a difference in the lives of others?
- Have I had fun and enjoyed life?
- Do I take pride in the legacy and name I have forged?

These are but five questions that ultimately are more important than our personal financial balance sheet.

Dad did not use the word "compassion." I doubt he even knew the word. However, in his own way, he explained to me what it meant far better than the dictionary explanation. When I returned home, I described the event to my mother. She smiled and said, "Always think what it must be like to walk in someone else's shoes."

Her point was that it is easy for someone to comment about the problems and behavior of others. Until you have similar experiences, you cannot understand what led to their actions. She continued with some advice: "You may be fortunate not to have had that particular problem, but put yourself in the same situation, and you will appreciate the difficulty that person encountered."

Value Learned: Not everyone may be as fortunate as you are. Be thankful you have the opportunity and means to be of assistance to others.

COURAGE

Stand up for what you believe
Courage is needed for you to achieve

When we hear the word "courage," we think of bravery. This is very true. Courage and bravery are connected. Courage is having the conviction that the action one is taking is correct, and the outcome will be positive. Bravery is implementing the conviction by means of action. Over the course of a lifetime, individuals encounter situations they have never faced. Both the pros and cons of decisions they must make are examined. At some point, the moment of truth arrives and it is decision time. Some individuals will back away and not make a decision. Some will rely on others to make a decision for them. The courageous and brave will step forward after considering available facts and advice and take action. If successful, one can take pride in the decision. If the decision was unsuccessful, you should not become discouraged, but learn from the experience. As a child, and until this very day, whenever I read or hear about a military hero, I think of how courageous that person had to be. I have the honor of being on the Board of the National Museum of Patriotism. This organization is dedicated to increasing awareness of the meaning, message, and mission of patriotism in America. Serving this organization has allowed me to become familiar with individuals that have earned our nation's highest military honor, the Congressional Medal of Honor. Each of their exploits defines the word "courage." As a youngster, I did associate courage with heroism. Whether it was a fictional character in a comic book or the brave hero in the movies or radio mysteries, all these were sources of courageous acts. Many of my relatives volunteered for military service and were viewed as courageous individuals. Jody's father gave his life for his country.

There are other examples that define the word "courage." My parents were adamant that people should speak up and express their feelings when the situation called for that type of action. They never understood why a person would remain silent when they had something to say. Later in life, I did understand what they were trying to teach was to have "the courage of your conviction."

Although my parents supported speaking your mind, they also tempered it with being respectful. This meant not demeaning the recipient of your comments. I remember a number of meetings in which I accompanied my mother and observed her behavior with friends and family. There was never any doubt as to her opinion on a variety of subjects. While I did understand the benefit of this trait, I found it very difficult to emulate. I believe this was a function of maturity, or perhaps it conflicted with another behavioral directive: "respect your elders." As I got older, my shyness diminished, and I realized the positive value of presenting one's view. The lesson of "stand up and be counted" has great merit. It serves as both a catharsis and an expression of your position and feelings. It is a very hollow feeling to wish you had said something after the opportunity has passed.

The next meaning of courage that I learned was exploring the unknown. This to me was overcoming the fear of failure. My dad and grandfather taught me to dream and try to fulfill the dream. I cannot imagine what was going through my father's mind when he bid his family farewell and left for "the New World." He was eighteen and was leaving familiar surroundings, family, and home. Setting off on a journey to an unknown place, he probably was unsure if he would ever see his family again. He embarked on that journey unaccompanied, without knowledge of English, money, education, or job prospects. All he had was a dream and courage.

He was but one of millions of that generation that made the effort and took the risk of exploring the unknown to realize their dream. Today, I smile when I'm driving in the neighborhood and see parents with their children awaiting the middle school bus.

Courage and risk are closely tied. It takes courage to risk something you deem to be precious. My dad taught me firsthand about having the courage to take some risks. At the age of fifteen, I wanted to sell souvenir football pins at the University of Minnesota football games. I needed one hundred dollars to buy materials, and asked my dad to lend me the money. His response was disappointing but interesting. He knew I had a savings account and asked how much was in the account. I told him the balance was $145. He then said if I really thought my idea was worthwhile, I should take a risk and have the courage to use my own money. It proved to be a wise and fortuitous decision. There were five home football games and I turned the $145 I put at risk into a net profit of $215. Needless to say, it was a boost in self-confidence. I thought I would become the first millionaire in our family. That was his risk versus reward lesson.

Several years later, I wanted to spend the summer in Chicago so I could enjoy the summer vacation with Jody. My dad asked how I was going to fund that adventure. His logic was impeccable as he detailed what the expenses would be for food, lodging, gas, and entertainment. He also was clear that I would have to get a summer job in Chicago, a place to live, and fund my own expenses.

He concluded the discussion with a question: "Do you think you can support yourself?" I told him yes, and off I went. Although there was skepticism expressed, I embarked on my journey with $150 and hopes of finding employment. I found a room at a YMCA for $11 a week. It had no maid service, and the showers were shared with other residents. The first thing I did the next morning was visit the industrial section along the Chicago River. I then started knocking on doors in search of a summer job. After several rejections, I did come upon a company that manufactured molasses. The manager in charge happened to be from Minnesota. When he learned that I was a student at the University of Minnesota, he became friendly and he offered me a maintenance position. My responsibility was painting the exterior of the building. That did not work out, so he reassigned me to learn how to be a pipe fitter. That also was not my area of expertise, so he thought I could work in the supply and parts area and maintain inventory control records. That proved to be a good decision for both of us. My take-home pay was $138 per week. Given my minimal expenses, I thought I was rich beyond belief. Both my family as well as Jody's suddenly began to believe that maybe I did have some potential. It was a fun summer and an experience that I shall always remember. In retrospect, this was another time Dad tested my courage.

One final example that fulfilled my dad's teaching occurred when I completed my military service. He asked what I planned to do for a career, and I responded that I was going to seek employment utilizing my education and skills. He offered me his business and said that I could build upon it. I thanked him but declined the offer. Tears welled in his eyes, and I tried to comfort him by expressing my appreciation and reasoning. The explanation I gave was that he demonstrated great courage by leaving Europe in his youth and achieved success with a beginning void of family, education, the English language, and any financial support. I in turn had the benefit of all these critical components and should be able to succeed without help. His response was he had tears not of sadness, but of pride that he had taught me well.

Over the years, there have been countless opportunities that have presented themselves—most of which have taken courage to experience. Fortunately, my dear wife Jody is not at all risk-averse. She is a role model for having the courage to explore the unknown. For example, at the age of eighteen, she left the security of her family and, with a group of other teens that she did not know, lived in Israel for the better part of a year. She exchanged the comfort and security of her home to work on a farm in a dangerous environment. The state of Israel was in its infancy at that time, and living conditions and safety made this adventure hazardous, to say the least.

There is yet another aspect of courage. While life is full of adventures, joy, and opportunities, at times it also is accompanied with problems, issues, and adversity.

It is during these times that courage is called for. Somewhere, somehow, some way, we must learn to face and cope with these situations. It takes great strength and courage to survive some of the problems that arise. The ability to overcome troubled times— and to continue to look for a ray of light as opposed to giving up in despair—is indeed at the core of courage.

As time passes, I have learned the value of courage. However, I have also learned that courage is not something that can be taken with reckless abandon. It is one thing to pursue a dream or take advantage of an opportunity. However, one must also understand that these same opportunities come with inherent risks. The adage "look before you leap" is very appropriate. There will be times when courage itself will not carry the day, but if one doesn't try, he or she will never know.

Value Learned: Make a decision and implement it. Do not contemplate, hesitate, or abdicate.

CREATIVITY

Putting forth something new
Says a great deal about you

In my youth, I never gave much thought to being creative. I had a chemistry set but never tried to experiment with anything that was not in the accompanying directions. I had the usual set of building blocks, play logs, and an erector set, but never tried to build something that was not already illustrated. I read story books, but didn't think about other stories to tell. My mom would make some unusual knitwear, my sister would try different recipes, and I had a cousin who experimented with assorted chemicals, and an uncle that was a successful entrepreneur. My wife, Jody, is very creative. She has custom-designed over a hundred baby quilts, which over the years have been wonderful and personalized baby gifts. However, I just did not think "outside the box."

In the military, the culture was one of "do what you're told," "follow orders," "refer to the manual or table of organization," and finally, "don't get creative." In retrospect, I understand the importance of this military mindset and clearly appreciate the reasoning for it.

My professional experience at IBM was one of a mixed culture. The company had some rules that were set in stone. However, the organization also recognized that it did not have a monopoly on brainpower. This was best illustrated by a poster the company created, which is now a collector's item. It has this famous quote from Mr. Thomas J. Watson Jr.: "We are convinced that any business needs its wild ducks, and in IBM, we try not to tame them." Wild ducks do and fly pretty much as they please. They function well without direction and arrive at their chosen destination. To survive, they have to be innovative and creative when it comes to locating a food supply or evading predators. They do perfectly well without being tamed or caged and forced to rely on assistance for survival. Similarly, intelligent, reliable, innovative employees should not be put in a restricted environment where their creativity and self-reliance is inhibited to the detriment of the organization. Subsequently, another balancing quote was put forth: "Even wild ducks fly in formation." Wild ducks understand the value of flying together and getting to their destination as a team. They understand there is strength in numbers—if they stray too far, it can very well jeopardize the entire group. An organization thrives best when there is teamwork and unity in achieving a specific goal. Chaos can occur when individuals engage in a power struggle and move in different directions.

I believe that, within everyone, there lies a reservoir of creativity. It just has to be ignited to fuel the fire. In my case, this occurred during a performance review. The evaluation was good, but not outstanding. My manager explained that although my performance was satisfactory, that was expected and was required to stay employed. He went on to explain that to excel, earn additional compensation, and be given more responsibility, it would be necessary to improve an existing process or develop something that would result in greater efficiencies. The translation was clear: "Come up with either something new or improve what is currently available."

The light went on! Also, reality set in. I was not an inventor, an artist, or musician. Neither was I a craftsman, engineer, playwright, author, or any one of a myriad of other professions and occupations. However, I believed sharing my interpersonal management and problem-solving skills and experience would tap into whatever creativity did exist. Also, if able to bring this thought to fruition, it would serve to be a source of self-satisfaction.

After retiring from IBM, I decided to do some volunteer activity and did some lecturing at Georgia State University. This experience was very rewarding from an intellectual viewpoint and allowed me to interact with a different generation and relate to a new and different set of challenges they were facing. My focus was how the human resource function had evolved in American industry.

My professional career began in 1959 and continues to this day. As I reflect on those fifty-seven years, significant changes have occurred. While my observations are generalizations, they are based upon ongoing experience.

Strategic versus tactical planning: There was a time when organizations were focused on strategic plans of three, five, or even ten years. Today, management may very well compare current performance by quarter, month, week, or even day to the comparable period the previous year.

A subtle but ongoing erosion of ethics has occurred. One can read daily examples of professions—be they commerce, athletics, politics, theology, education, science, medicine, or the public sector to name some—in which either groups or individuals have made questionable ethical decisions. While this may not be a new phenomenon, it appears to be more invasive.

Innovation and technology have reached incredible speeds, resulting in never-before-seen efficiencies. Ideas that were only dreams have become reality. Expenses have declined, profits are record breaking, and productivity has soared.

The human resource function presents an interesting dichotomy. On the positive side, employees are very well-qualified, competent, and energized. From a negative perspective, the allegiance and loyalty is not what it once was.

The perception of human resources has undergone a significant transition. In the past, employees were viewed as an investment. Both the employer and the employee entered into what was expected to be a career-long relationship. Longevity was considered a given. It was common for individuals to work for one employer for thirty or more years, retire, enjoy their pension, and watch the sunset. Today, it is not uncommon for an individual to have five or more employment experiences, focus on maximizing his or her earnings so he or she can retire early someday, and live off of his or her investments and stock options.

Today, many employees are viewed as commodities rather than investments. Whatever the current market conditions dictate will have great influence on what human resource actions management elects to implement. In the past, loyalty was typically mutual—today, it is far less so.

This experience led me into a new and different direction—consulting. In a consultative capacity, I was fortunate to utilize my professional background and experience to assist different organizations with human resource issues. This also allowed and required taking a creative approach to earn trust and confidence of clients to successfully solve problems. Creativity is most essential to achieve success when you enter an environment of diverse opinions, views, and positions.

While creativity is beneficial to developing solutions and innovation, it also has another valuable dimension—it can serve to be a learning and development tool to leave behind for others to utilize. With that in mind, I decided to visit the "creative well" once again.

Over the many years of my professional career, I encountered a multitude of management issues. While these were both challenging and interesting, there existed a central theme to each. That theme was the demeanor, behavior, and overall professionalism that a successful manager should strive to portray. Many words have been written, lectures given, and visual and audio tapes produced to address this subject.

I have tried to distill volumes into what I consider to be seven critical and essential management characteristics:

1. HAVE INTEGRITY and HONESTY
2. BE BRAVE
3. REMAIN CALM
4. HAVE COMPASSION
5. THINK AHEAD
6. LISTEN
7. HAVE A POSITIVE ATTITUDE

Many more certainly can be added to these seven. All would have merit. I wanted to impart these values to others and decided to use some creativity by designing a perpetual calendar. A poetic rhyme was written to describe each characteristic. The rhyme is portrayed with a drawing to depict its meaning. A walnut stand was designed to hold the calendar. The item served to remind the recipient each month of a valuable management characteristic. It was copyrighted in 1994 and has served my intent to leave something for others in a creative way.

Value Learned: Creativity is a distinguishing characteristic that enhances productivity.

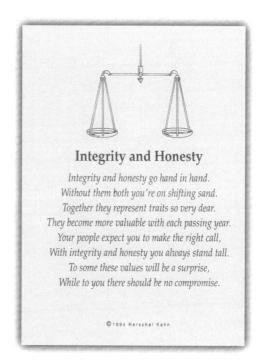

Integrity and Honesty

Integrity and honesty go hand in hand.
Without them both you're on shifting sand.
Together they represent traits so very dear.
They become more valuable with each passing year.
Your people expect you to make the right call,
With integrity and honesty you always stand tall.
To some these values will be a surprise,
While to you there should be no compromise.

© 1994 Herschel Kahn

Be Brave

In the face of fire, don't back away.
Be brave, speak out and lead the way.
You're not alone in the position you take.
To avoid tough issues is a mistake.
Stand up, let other people know what you believe.
Their admiration and respect you will receive.
Being brave is a leaders' trait.
It serves as the key to open the gate
Through which we can walk with pride.
Far better to be brave than try to hide.

©1994 Herschel Kahn

Remain Calm

Remaining calm is not easy to do
When your people are upset and looking at you.
Don't be nervous and don't be tense,
Be the one to show some sense.
Remain calm and lead the way.
Pretty soon you will hear them say,
"If only we had kept our poise
Instead of making all that noise".
To scream and shout does no good,
For if it did we all would.
Remain calm and lead the way.
You will solve the problem and save the day.

©1994 Herschel Kahn

Compassion

There is a time to show your strength
And stand against the tide.
There also is another time to show a softer side.
The leader who cannot shed a tear
And has a heart of stone.
May be someone all do fear,
But is also all alone.
Showing compassion is something that is not hard to do,
Remember troubled times can also come to you.
Today can be sunny, tomorrow filled with rain,
At that point in time, compassion eases the pain.

© 1994 Herschel Kahn

Think Ahead

Looking back is simple for you.
Thinking ahead is hard to do.
It's important to stop and think things through.
For a leader must take a forward view
To stay ahead of the rest of the pack,
Don't waste time looking back.
Anticipating problems before they arise
Will surely prevent an unpleasant surprise.
When you think ahead, the future is today.
If you do that, at the top you will stay.

© 1994 Herschel Kahn

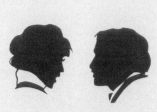

A Listener Be

When someone is speaking, a listener be,
As that is a sign of maturity.
It's harder to listen than it is to hear
For listening is a skill that makes things clear.
When people send a thought our way,
Know there is something they want to convey.
To listen is the least we can do,
Remember their message is directed to you.

©1994 Herschel Kahn

Positive Attitude

As we journey along our paths each day,
We encounter obstacles that make us say,
"Why are these challenges so very tall?
How will I ever scale this wall?"
That's the time we must look within
And say to ourselves, we certainly can win.
Our strength and resolve will carry us through
Seas that are rough and skies that aren't blue.
A positive attitude will help us believe
There is nothing at all we cannot achieve.

©1994 Herschel Kahn

EDUCATION

To arrive at your destination
The key is to obtain an education

My dad had no formal education. He was raised in a peasant environment in rural Russia. His father taught him some very basic language and survival skills. He did receive some religious training to learn prayers and customs. However, his primary responsibility was assisting his parents with whatever was needed to provide food and shelter for the family. I will forever remember his explanation of why he journeyed to America. To avoid conscription into the Russian army of Czar Nicholas II, fathers had one of two choices: they could either scrape up enough money to send their son to the "New World" or amputate an index finger so the young man would be unable to fire a rifle, thereby being disqualified from military service. Fortunately, my grandfather was able to send his son to America. Upon arrival, he—as so many immigrants before him had—learned English from friends or relatives, as well as some basic math and reading skills. He found a job making picture frames and went on to lead a very productive and satisfying life.

Mom was more fortunate. She was born in Minneapolis and attended a primary school and then a vocational high school to learn bookkeeping skills. Higher education was not an option, as she worked and contributed to the support of her family.

While my parents had no formal education, they had deep respect for its value and were determined that my sister and I would have the opportunity to attend college. With the opportunity came the responsibility to graduate. This was clearly understood, and there would be no further or alternative discussion.

As a child, I never thought about education. Going to school was understood. The instructions were pay attention, behave, do your homework, and be on time. Off I went each day, following in the footsteps of my older sister.

In elementary school, I was far more interested in learning how to play baseball than multiplication tables. In middle school, I found the 1945 World Series between the Chicago Cubs and Detroit Tigers more interesting than either algebra or geometry. High school brought the ultimate question: What possible value could ever ensue from having to memorize the prologue to Chaucer's *Canterbury Tales*? Years later, I learned this tidbit endeared me to my future mother-in-law, as she thought her daughter found a most cultured and educated beau.

It was a slow maturation process for me before I started realizing the value of education. I began to understand what my mother kept preaching to me as a youngster. Her message was, "Go to school, study hard, learn something, and someday you will be happy you did." One of my incentives was to earn enough money to enjoy a quality life. I was able to comprehend the pathway to that goal required a skill set and educational background that would allow me to compete for a position providing such an opportunity. The fact the majority of my peers were planning to attend college also served as further motivation.

I began to understand that education is more than sitting in a classroom. It is a process of developing the skills, interests, and abilities that will facilitate the realization of hopes, dreams, and ultimate potential. It is not necessarily a diploma or degree. It may come in a variety of forms. Examples would include certificates, licenses, self-taught courses, reading, or specific course training. I have ultimate respect for a physician, a carpenter, a teacher, a mechanic, an electrician or an electrical engineer, an information technology developer, or a painter. Each person has a skill and ability that has been brought to the surface through some form of education or training.

Georgia State University
University Plaza • Atlanta, Georgia 30303-3083

Herschel Kahn
Adjunct Professor and Executive in Residence
W.T. Beebe Institute of Personnel
and Employment Relations

College of Business Administration

Office: 404/651-2792
Home: 404/642-5460

Education has no boundaries. It is not uncommon for an individual to have an interest in a particular course of study and upon completion decide to pursue an entirely different career path. Knowledge has no expiration date. One of our daughters was very interested in and earned a degree in anthropology. She found it to be a very challenging course of study, but upon graduation, decided to pursue an entirely different career path. She had a very successful career working for a multinational company in the hospitality industry. When asked why she didn't utilize her anthropology education, her response was, "I thought it would be fun as well as interesting."

As I enter my twilight years, it is my firm conviction that education is ongoing. As a youth, I couldn't wait for summer vacation and being away from the classroom. In college, I was eager to graduate and start my career. I envisioned being free of schedules, projects, and lectures. My first week in the military brought me back to reality. It didn't take long for me to realize that education is a lifelong process. Eleven years after graduating from the University of Minnesota, I thought a graduate degree would enhance my career opportunities. After three years of evening and weekend classes, I did earn an MBA from DePaul University. The effort reinforced to me the value of education.

It is my firm belief that continuing the pursuit of knowledge is of immense value. It takes many forms that are not necessarily in the classroom. Examples include reading books or periodicals, hearing lectures, taking classes to hone skills, working puzzles, or researching information of subjects for which we have acquired an interest.

MBA from DePaul University

As with everything in life, education comes with a price. Financial consideration aside, there are in my opinion nine other attributes that one must have to reach his or her goal:

ENTHUSIASM
Be enthusiastic about the journey you are about to commence. One must want to succeed and not go through the motions to please someone else.

DEDICATION
As with anything one considers worthwhile, there needs to be commitment on your part to see the journey through both good and difficult times.

UNYIELDING
There will be times when you may question whether the effort is worth the reward. You must be able to ignore distractions and put forth the energy required to overcome any obstacle.

COURAGE
You may question your ability to undertake a specific educational goal. Muster the strength and will to move forward, and prove to yourself and others you can and will succeed.

ACCEPTANCE
Starting the process can be easy and fun. However, accept the fact there will be times when the thought of giving up will cross your mind. Know success requires perseverance.

TENACITY

Whenever the thought of abandoning your goal occurs, you must forge ahead to overcome any deterrents standing in your way.

INVESTMENT

View this activity as an investment in the future. The dividends will flow back to you with significant interest as your future unfolds.

OPPORTUNITY

Equipped with education and training, numerous opportunities will become available.

NEVER ENDING

Each day presents an opportunity to learn something new or improve upon something we already know. The process is without end.

ETHICS

Right versus wrong is known by all
Ethical behavior allows one to stand tall

Doing the "right" thing was a subject of conversation I remember from my earliest childhood days. The word "ethics" was never used, and it was not until later in life that I understood what was meant by the "right" thing. Reflecting on my early years, I recall a situation my maternal grandfather, two uncles, and my dad were discussing one evening. I remember the time period was during the 1940s. During that time frame, my grandfather collected scrap iron and sold it to dealers, who in turn would resell it to smelters to be used for manufacturing new steel. Scrap iron was a valuable commodity during the Second World War. The discussion that I was listening to involved a decision my grandfather made. He had a contract to deliver a set quantity of scrap metal at a fixed price. After signing an agreement with a set price, the value of scrap iron soared. The dealer with whom the contract was negotiated recognized that my grandfather would deliver the metal at a loss rather than a profit. For this reason, he offered to renegotiate the contract to ensure my grandfather would not lose any money. My grandfather refused the offer and was very emphatic in explaining his position that an agreement must be honored regardless of personal gain or loss. The words he kept repeating were "doing the right thing is more valuable that money." It was a lesson that I always remembered.

Some thirty-five years later, the lesson was reinforced. I had the responsibility of collecting past-due payments for IBM typewriters.

My manager would analyze my performance each week. One day, he asked why a particular client did not remit his payments for several months. I explained that I was in constant communication with the individual and that he would continually complain about the quality of the machine. When it was properly serviced, only then would he pay what was due. The manager said we needed to visit the gentleman's office immediately. I suggested that it would not be a prudent use of his time to make a personal visit to one customer about one machine. That suggestion was to no avail, and within a few minutes, we were in a taxi traveling to visit the client.

During the ride, my manager said, "You are going to learn something valuable today."

We arrived at the office and were greeted by the customer. The IBM executive asked, "What can our company do to satisfy you?"

The customer replied, "I just want this machine serviced so that it will perform properly."

My manager replied, "Will you be happy if we replaced this typewriter with a new one?"

The customer said, "Why would you do that? I have used this one for almost two years."

The manager said, "Our company stands behind all its products, and we want happy customers. For that reason, a new replacement typewriter will arrive before the day is over."

On our return trip to the office, I questioned the economics of his decision and immediately received a lesson on the right thing to do. That customer will always remain a customer. Doing the right thing cannot be related to monetary gain but rather long-term goodwill.

LESSON FROM A STRANGER

It is true the majority of the values we have learned result from our interaction with our family, friends, teachers, clergy, business associates, and reading, as well as other sources. However, a perfect stranger can also serve to teach a value we will forever treasure.

The year was 1957. Jody and I were residing in Rochefort, France. I was the post quartermaster officer, and Jody was teaching at the school for children of military personnel located on the base. During the winter holiday season, the two of us—together with two other schoolteachers—decided to drive from southern France to Edinburgh, Scotland. We drove to our departure point in France and boarded a ferry to transport our vehicle and the four of us to Dover, England. Upon arrival in England, we proceeded to drive north to Scotland. About twenty miles into the trip, we experienced a flat tire. I changed the tire and continued twenty miles when another flat tire occurred. Having no other spare tire, I made a decision to leave the automobile and solicit assistance from any passing vehicle. The night was quite dark, it was a Saturday evening, and traffic was extremely light. After waiting about twenty minutes, a motorist seeing the situation did stop. The driver was a very well-dressed gentleman. He asked if he could be of assistance and offered to drive me about fifteen miles farther down the road where he knew of a service station that could provide me with a new tire. I thanked him and off we went. During the trip, I asked where he was going, and he replied that he was on his way to attend a social gathering. After buying a new tire, I thanked him and said I would await someone going in the other direction for my return trip to the stranded passengers. He insisted on returning me to our car.

I said, "Thanks for the offer, but you already are late for your event, and I certainly don't want to delay you further."

He was determined to take me back and did so. Once there he proceeded to help me change the tire. Not only was he going to be late for his event, but also his appearance after changing the tire was not as pristine as it was earlier. Before he left, I offered him some money for his kindness and trouble. He absolutely would not accept anything. I asked for his contact information, and he also declined that request.

He then explained his actions most succinctly: "If it were not for you Yanks, there would be no England today." He then went on to vividly recall the events of the bombing of London by

Germany during 1942–1944. He continued by saying, "I promised myself that if I ever had an opportunity to help an American, I would go to any end to do so. You, sir, have fulfilled my wish. He drove away, and I never again had contact with that Good Samaritan. It was quite a lesson in ethical behavior. In his mind, he was doing what he thought to be the right thing.

Ethical behavior is a key ingredient to a properly functioning society. Rarely does a day pass without the media advising us of ethical breaches both in the public and private sectors. Whether they are athletes, teachers, clergy, politicians, doctors, lawyers, business executives, or others in positions of trust, the question can be asked, "Where were they when this value was taught?"

Value Learned: If you make a promise, keep your word, even if it's just to yourself.

FAITH

Faith is an individual's choice
Recognize there may be a higher voice

During my lifetime, I have had the opportunity to observe, meet, and interact with literally thousands of people. One of the greatest benefits of this privilege was to gain an appreciation and understanding that individuals embrace and observe different faiths, beliefs, and customs. What is paramount is the ability to appreciate and accept their choice of faith. Whatever that choice may be, it belongs to the individual.

From my personal perspective, it is my belief a higher power does exist. When I look at a beautiful flower and admire the intricate shape and design, I can't help feeling that man alone could never recreate such a beautiful object. When I admire the vivid colors of fall foliage, I feel a power greater than man is at work. The miracle of life itself, that no two individuals are identical, reinforces my belief. Situations have occurred in my personal life that confirm a higher power has a master plan. I think of the circumstances that brought Jody and me together. I never envisioned bringing a grandson as a child from a foreign country to raise in our home. I never planned to work for a multinational corporation for thirty-three years. The list is without end. Each of the examples cited exemplify unplanned events. There are times when we can establish a goal, devise a plan to achieve the goal, and implement the plan so the objective is met. In my youth, I did think that someday I hoped to marry, have a good career, and someday be a grandfather. Each of those things did occur through a power beyond my control. I often ask the question of myself, "Why did a basketball go off the court and bounce to Jody? Of all the corporations in America, why was IBM located next door to the building occupied by my former employer? Why did my son decide to work in Honduras and marry a Honduran woman with the end result that our family assumed the responsibility of raising and caring for our only grandchild?" These examples serve to reinforce my belief that a higher power does exist. I view that belief as having a direct connection to my religious faith. Regardless of the denomination, faith can account for many things. Each event serves to strengthen my belief. I have had many experiences, some good and some not so good. However, upon reflection, each one served a purpose. People may have a different perspective. I am most respectful of their prerogative to do so.

"A higher power created this flower."
A hobby of mine was to grow flowers and enter
them competitively in the Southeastern Flower Show.
This is my first-place award.

Whatever path of faith a person elects to pursue is his or her decision. After traveling the world, I have witnessed multiple examples of devotion to various faiths. I have seen natives worshiping flowers, other individuals the sun, various idols, and birds. Jody and I have visited churches, mosques, temples, shrines, synagogues, and mountains throughout the world. Each serves as a place to observe one's faith. I have deep appreciation and respect for whatever belief anyone selects. I ask for the same appreciation and respect for my choice. I have concluded the source of many problems stems from one faith attempting to impose its belief on another.

I take great pride in my Jewish heritage. The centerpiece of Judaism is the Torah. The Torah is the most important text of Judaism. The first five books of the Bible and the Ten Commandments are contained therein. My parents, grandparents, and great-grandparents were all Jewish. Growing up in a Jewish home, I only knew about my religion and faith. Our home was in a Jewish enclave in North Minneapolis. Neighbors, friends, schoolmates, and shopkeepers were predominately Jewish. The synagogue, Hebrew school recreation center, and shops were within walking distance. It wasn't until I reached middle school that I realized a bigger universe did exist. My parents implemented a culture to ensure that I would embrace Judaism and never stray from its precepts.

Lesson number one: I was enrolled in the Minneapolis Talmud Torah. This school taught not only the Hebrew language, but also Jewish history, culture, rituals, and Bible study. Classes were scheduled 4:00 to 6:00 p.m. Monday through Thursday and 9:00 a.m. to 12:00 p.m. on Sunday morning. This training regimen was not optional, but in my parents' minds, obligatory. I was not exactly excited with the requirement but understood the home organization chart and complied, although reluctantly. After a full day of public school and then going to another school for religious training, one could expect behavior problems from nine-year-old boys. Those expectations were not only met but were greatly exceeded. This was not the happiest part of my young life, but it continued until my sixteenth birthday.

My uncle Ben, my sister Harriet,
and me at my bar mitzvah

The lesson my parents were teaching that I did not comprehend until later in life was to understand, practice, and perpetuate my Jewish heritage. Both my mom and dad stressed the fact that I did not have to pursue a rabbinical career. However, as an adult, I would appreciate and feel comfortable in a Jewish environment and would continue to pass the tradition to succeeding generations. They were absolutely correct. Sometimes, lessons taught do not become meaningful until the passage of time. I view it as my responsibility to continue practicing and teaching my faith to succeeding generations.

My ancestors diligently observed our religion. They sacrificed greatly to ensure their descendants continued observing their faith. Judaism is one of the great religions of the world. Without personal commitment, the culture and proud heritage would cease to exist. I

accept it as an honor, privilege, and obligation to continue its per-
petuation. In my opinion, this dedication is necessary for every religion.

With maturity comes understanding. Looking back at this
period of my life, I recall one particular event that my dad and I
laughed about in later years. My mother maintained a kosher home.
I was taught that Jewish people do not under any circumstances
eat any pork product. My father emphasized this precept over and
over. To illustrate the point, he used as an example that pork
products could very well contain a "worm." This worm could
enter your body and navigate to the point where your arm joins
your shoulder, and one day when shaving, your arm could just
fall off in the washbasin. Clearly, he was referring to trichinosis
with more than a bit of exaggeration. He was successful, however,
in planting the wisdom of abstaining from eating pork. Years later
while in an ROTC summer camp, I was in a field situation where
ham was served for the evening meal. I declined and ate lettuce
and beans. The next evening, ham was served again. I asked the
platoon leader if there was anything else on the menu. With a look
of disdain, he reminded me this was the army, not a gourmet
restaurant. The third evening meal consisted once again of ham.
At that point, I was quite hungry, looked around, and noticed
there were twenty-five fellow cadets, all gentile, and all of whom
had two arms. The ham dinner that evening was most tasteful,
and I still have both arms. When I shared that story with my dad
we both could hardly stop laughing. It is my opinion there comes
a time when common sense and practical judgement must be
exercised in decision making. While I don't condone a "pick and
choose" approach, which may lead to a slippery slope, I do think
there are occasions where discretion can be practiced.

As a child, I never gave much thought to faith. As the years passed,
the realization set in that something other than perseverance
alone would allow me to utilize whatever potential I possessed.
Life is a road that has twists and turns. It has hills and valleys.
There are places that are straight and the sun is shining. There are
times when the road is slippery, dark, and strewn with obstacles.

Something other than cruise control, a GPS, and a full tank of fuel is needed to reach your destination. I have determined that something for me has been faith.

Faith has played an important part in my life. If people believe that things "just happen," that is clearly their prerogative. Some people believe in luck, destiny, or astrology—the choice is for them to make. The genesis of many conflicts is thought to have originated from faith or lack thereof. I believe faith can also serve as a source of strength and comfort.

Value Learned: Faith has been a most important part of my life. It is very personal, and respect must be shown for people of all faiths, as well as for those who choose to "go it alone."

FAMILY

A loving family can't be beat
Being together is life's great treat

Love and devotion to family were brought home to me as one of my earliest childhood recollections. At the time, I did not realize the lesson that was being taught. However, as I grew older, the genesis of this most important value became clear.

My dad left his family in Kovno, Russia, at the age of seventeen. He arrived in the "New World" on January 1, 1900. The family he left behind consisted of two brothers, two sisters, and his parents. He worked at various jobs and saved enough to bring one brother to join him in Minneapolis. The two men continued to work until they could afford to bring their parents and siblings to America. The brothers provided for their family and welcomed two additional brothers and two more sisters born in the United States. My dad and uncle represented the total source of support for the entire family. When the material needs of the family were secure, only then my father thought of his personal future. My dad was the eldest of his siblings. He accepted the responsibility of taking care of his family. Only after they were all provided for was a home established and a business founded. He married at the age of forty-eight. After his marriage, he and his brother continued to provide whatever assistance their parents and younger siblings required.

My maternal grandparents had eight children, all of whom lived in the same household. They pooled their resources and, together, contributed to the support of the family unit. One by one, as each child left the household to make his or her own life, he or she continued to support the entire family, ensuring all were cared for.

My kids

Communication and interaction were the next building blocks that formed the foundation upon which the importance of family was built. At least three times a week, my mom and dad would visit my grandparents, who resided nearby. They would sit around the kitchen table discussing current events, people they liked or disliked, politics, and sometimes other family members. It was not uncommon for my parents and grandparents to converse in Yiddish. Upon reflection, I believe this occurred for two reasons. The first being that my grandparents were more comfortable speaking Yiddish as that was their native tongue, and English was not all that familiar for them. This was especially the case for my grandmother. Secondly, there were certain subjects they determined would be better discussed beyond children's ears. As time went by, I began to understand the topics included neighbors, relatives within the family, President Roosevelt, and synagogue members, including the rabbi.

Perhaps one of the most memorable examples of what family meant to my father was the relationship he had with his brother. They were partners in a furniture business for their entire adult lives. The interesting financial arrangement they had was the creation of one company checking account. All funds received from the business were deposited into that one account. My dad had a family, a home, children, and significant other expenses associated with the care of his family. His brother never married, resided in an apartment above their place of business, lived in a most frugal manner, and had miniscule expenses. Approximately 90 percent of the business net income was directed to my dad's requirements. At one point, I discussed with him what I thought to be a most unusual financial arrangement. His answer said it all: **"We're brothers"**. They worked together every day for sixty years, and never once was there a discussion between them about money. First and foremost in my father's life was family. His entire life was dedicated and committed to the welfare of his family. Sharing and caring were two fundamental precepts of his life. Nothing was more important to him than family. The meaning he was conveying with that statement was whatever the business had was theirs, not his. Although he was a staunch believer in free enterprise and capitalism, when it came to family, he was comfortable with the philosophy "contribute to your ability, take according to your need."

The second example that reinforced the value family meant to my parents concerned my mom. Not a day would pass that she did not have a phone conversation with her mother. Also, more often than not, she would have conversations on a daily basis with at least one brother or sister. When her youngest sister was diagnosed with a terminal illness, Mom would visit the hospital every day. She didn't drive and made the trip by streetcar.

Another example of family devotion concerned fresh eggs. My parents thought store-bought eggs were not as fresh as those one could get from a poultry farm. For that reason, my dad would take me and drive on Sunday mornings to a chicken hatchery located about twenty-five miles outside of Minneapolis. On arrival, he would visit with the owner, then take me on a tour of the incubators to watch the baby chicks and visit the farm so I could see some of the animals. The main reason for the trip was to purchase ten dozen fresh eggs. When we returned home, he would, together with my mom, visit family members and give them fresh eggs. Sharing with family was an important part of their lives.

OUR CHILDREN

The four most wonderful, valuable, and precious gifts Jody and I have ever been privileged to receive are our four children. Each one is unique. There is a Yiddish word of Hebrew origin, *nachas*. Its meaning basically is having joy or pride from one's children. That is not to say that the word excludes childless parents because it clearly can have broader meaning as well. It is customary that when a child is born, a goodwill blessing is often extended to the parents: "You shall have much *nachas* from your child."

Our eldest is Louis. Born in France while we were in the service, he was the center of our universe. He has incredible mechanical skills, which is a complete mystery to us, since I have difficulty understanding which end of a screwdriver to use. It is amazing to see him disassemble an engine, have parts strewn hither and yon, and yet put the unit back together and have it run in superb fashion. His love of animals is wonderful to see and has kept our household supplied with pets for over fifty years.

Next came Michele. She was the perfect "little lady"—liked dolls, clothes, and jewelry—and always seemed happy. Her career path led to a most outstanding career in retail sales for a very upscale retail establishment. Year after year, her accomplishments have earned significant recognition.

Our third jewel is Hannah. As a child, she was extremely decisive and knew exactly what she wanted and would not be deterred. Her intellect is beyond description, and I have yet to encounter a problem that she could not solve. Hannah had a very successful marketing career with a prominent international hospitality organization. She currently is part of a consulting group with marketing responsibilities for hospitality property renovations. The world of electronics and computer technology has swept past me—without her, I would be adrift in a turbulent sea. She is devoted to raising our grandson Sam, and her dedication and commitment to that effort is beyond description.

Finally, we have Ben. He was a typical mischievous little boy. Jody has said on more than one occasion, "If he was our first, he would have been the last." Ben is a free spirit. He enjoys the outdoors. He prefers the space of Colorado and the open territory of Arizona to the large city lifestyle. He is extremely sociable and has a vast network of friends. He loves adventure and is perfectly happy sharing his lifestyle with his close pal, his dog Winston. He once counseled me that I have had a boring life in that I got out of college in four years, had one job for thirty-three years, one wife for over fifty years, and he had never seen me drunk. My retort that I was sorry to set such an example went unanswered.

The cycle of offspring maturation is one of life's great events. I fondly recall, when a tooth fell out of one of my children's mouths, putting it under his or her pillow at night with a dollar and telling him or her in the morning the "tooth fairy" left it. Now they accompany me to doctor's appointments. The memory of teaching them how to ride a bicycle is fresh in my mind. Now, with respect and sensitivity, they prefer to drive their parents during evening hours. As children, they were constantly reminded to take their vitamins or cough medicine. Now, they ensure our meds are put out each day and remind us to take them. It was common to remind them to dress warmly before leaving the house. Now, the question they ask is, "Are you sure you don't need a sweater? It's cold out there."

The transition from infancy to childhood, then adolescence and adulthood, is ongoing and relentless. Bringing each baby home from the hospital doesn't seem that long ago. Where have the years gone? We have indeed been blessed with *nachas*.

Three generations: Ben, me, Louis, and Sam

At times, love and dedication to family can be a source of friction in a marriage. This can occur when one partner does not have the same level of commitment as the other. Fortunately, I have been blessed with a wife who embraces the value I place on family relationships. Jody grew up surrounded by a loving family. She lost her father in World War II. She, her mother, and brother were living in Indianapolis, and following this great loss, relocated to be with family in Chicago. There was an immediate bond with her maternal relatives. The result was a high level of emotional support and outpouring of love to help ease the pain of their loss.

It was quite natural that as a family we forged strong relationships and family ties. Our dedication and belief in family unity was challenged by a situation that we never anticipated. While working in Honduras, our son met and married a Honduran woman. For personal reasons, our son returned to the United States and was not present when his wife gave birth to a son on February 19, 1998. Since our son was not present, we provided financial assistance to our daughter-in-law and grandson. In 2002 Jody and I traveled to Honduras to meet our extended family for the first time. While we were elated to meet and hold our grandson for the very first time, we were saddened to witness the quality of life they were enduring. On the flight home, we looked at each other and mutually agreed that we had to do something that would remedy the situation. Hence, the journey to bring mother and son to the United States complying completely with all immigration laws began.

Suffice it to say, having gone through that experience, we understand and appreciate how very difficult it is to come to our country legally. On August 12, 2004, we met our grandson Samuel Francisco Kahn and his mother Maria as they arrived in Atlanta. It was a thrill and a dream come true. The reality of the responsibility before us was expected but underestimated. A few of some obstacles we faced included language, education, socioeconomic background, culture and religion. There are no words that can do justice in describing the stress, strain, and struggle that fell upon

65

all parties as a result of the initiative we undertook. This was a life-changing event to the highest degree for everyone.

Sam and Grandpa

Once here, phase two began. The bureaucracy of obtaining a social security card and work permit for Maria had to be overcome. We made a decision to have our daughter Hannah named as Sam's guardian. This was yet another frustrating experience requiring interaction with the public sector. Finding an apartment and bilingual school was also a challenge. At this time, our son reentered the picture, and there were some adjustments involved with that occurrence. Thankfully, our family worked together to achieve our goal. We wanted to provide a pathway for our grandson to fully utilize all his abilities and skills—to have the opportunity to achieve his ultimate potential which otherwise would not be available to him.

At this writing, it has been eleven years since Sam and Maria joined our family.

The progress report is glowing and does not reflect the effort, pain, sweat, and tears put forth by Jody and Hannah and the support when called upon from our daughter Michele.

Sam is now eighteen. He stands six foot four inches, weighs 180 pounds, and is quite handsome. His English is perfect, he is very athletic and plays basketball and baseball, and he is quite social and has many friends. When he was thirteen, he had his bar mitzvah and delivered a speech that brought tears to the eyes of the congregation. Sam has traveled to Europe and Central America on youth trips. Hannah remains his guardian. Both Sam and Hannah live in our home. His parents are together and live in a condo ten minutes away with their three pets. They are included in all family events and have constant contact with Sam. Maria has a full-time job, and her English is coming along well. His dad has a full-time job and is an excellent truck mechanic. Sam is loved by his Aunt Michele and Uncle Ben.

This experience has been a test of endurance, patience, and love. There have been days when our private thoughts challenge the wisdom of our decision. While Jody and I will not witness the end result, we take great comfort and pride in knowing the role our family has played in shaping Sam's life. This has been a prime example of what a family can accomplish when presented with a challenge to determine if love triumphs over sacrifice.

Value Learned: The welfare of your family should be your first priority.

Sam's high school graduation, May 2016.
He has come a long way from the Honduran jungle.

My family

Favors

Doing someone a favor is our obligation
It need not be discussed in future conversation

At one time or another, everyone has had an opportunity to show kindness to someone without any expectation of a reward. When we help others, we believe it is the right thing to do. Perhaps in the back of our mind, we think that someday maybe the person we helped will return the favor to us. Where do we learn about helping others? At an early age, we learned about "The Golden Rule." Hopefully our parents, teachers, friends, siblings, and relatives at some point reinforced this behavior.

I observed many of my family at various times do favors for others. However, one particular experience made me look at a favor from an entirely different perspective. Before getting engaged, I had a talk with my dad about diamond rings. I knew absolutely nothing about jewelry, and Dad didn't know much more.

After our discussion, he asked me to come with him while he looked through very old files and notebooks. He came upon a tattered paper yellowed with age that had one name written on it. He handed me the paper and told me the person whose name was on the paper lived in Chicago and was in the jewelry business. He then suggested I call the gentleman and introduce myself as the son of Sam Kahn from Minneapolis. Evidently, I looked quite puzzled, and Dad asked if I had a problem with his suggestion.

I said, "Chicago is a very large city, and all I have is a name, no address or phone number."

The response I received was "If you want something, you will figure out how to get it."

I had some additional questions—for example, "How do you know this man? When did you last see or talk with him? What do I say in the event I do reach him?"

Dad said he had not spoken to or seen this gentleman in at least thirty-five years. He further said the rest of my questions were not important. He then wished me luck with the assignment.

A friend's appreciation

I was quite nervous about making the call but somehow summoned the courage to dial the number. After what seemed like forever, the man I wished to speak with did come to the phone. I was very relieved to know that at least he was still alive. I introduced myself and referenced my dad. The gentleman, to my great surprise, clearly remembered Dad and asked about him and how he was doing. After a pleasant exchange of information, I explained the purpose of my call. Simply put, I was seeking information about buying a diamond engagement ring. I readily admitted that I didn't know anything about the subject and that my dad suggested I reach out to him for assistance.

He was very warm and cordial and congratulated me on my forthcoming marriage. He then said he had a few questions to ask. Fortunately, I did know the answer to the first question, which was, "Do you know the 'cut' of the diamond your fiancée has chosen?"

I answered with great confidence, "Marquise."

At that point, he started to explain the quality criteria of diamonds. He then said he would send a selection of quality stones to me for examination and choice.

At that point, I was speechless. He asked why I had no comment, and I remember saying, "You don't know me and you're going to send me some diamonds? I find that hard to believe."

He was quite calm and said, "Don't worry, I know your father and I'm sure you are quite like him." I then asked about price, to which he responded, "Don't concern yourself with price, just pick the stone you both are happy with." He asked for the correct delivery address and said a package would arrive within the next two days. I thanked him over and over, and that was the extent of the conversation.

Two days later, true to his word, the package containing the diamonds arrived. We selected one particular stone. I called the gentleman again and told him we made our choice and the other stones were on the way back to him.

He said, "Fine, glad you are pleased, and I wish you a long and happy marriage."

I thanked him and asked again about the cost of the stone. One more time, he said that I should not be concerned about cost.

I immediately went to my dad and told him the entire story. He had no comment other than that he was glad all went well. I pressed my dad on what was all this about. How could this person after all those many years just send something that valuable without the slightest concern about money? I then asked a very pointed question to my father: "Dad, what is the story? Does he owe you for something you once did for him?"

Dad's reply was, "You really don't need an answer to your question, so there will be no further discussion."

We invited the jeweler to our wedding. At the reception. I asked him the same question I asked my dad. His response was, "I respect your dad greatly, and let's leave it at that."

Seventeen years went by, and shortly before my dad passed on, I asked him one more time about his relationship with the jeweler. His answer was "Herschel, if you ever do a favor for someone and talk about it, it no longer is a favor." I never did and never will know the entire story. However, I did learn when a favor is not a favor.

A favor is a nonobligatory act of kindness done freely without being asked. It is not a favor when it is in response to a request. If we are asked, for example, "Do me a favor and," it is no longer voluntary. At that point, we can accept or reject the request. The primary difference is a voluntary self-initiated act versus complying with a request. When doing a favor, the giver typically expects nothing in return. It is a gesture offered in the spirit of help, assistance, and kindness. If a favor is requested, more often than not a *quid pro quo* is also offered. For example, "Lend me some money and I'll pay you back with interest." If one discusses the act, he or she may very well be seeking praise by calling attention to themselves that they are kind, sensitive, caring, or benevolent. The recipient of a favor may very well not want the event made public. In that instance, the act may be self-serving rather than a genuine act of kindness.

Value Learned: When given an opportunity to do a favor, take the initiative, make the offer, and let it remain personal and confidential. It no longer is a favor if disclosed to others.

Forgiveness

Forgiving is not easy to do
Remaining angry has no value

"To err is human. To forgive is divine," "Forgive and forget," "Turn the other cheek," "Forgive them, for they know not what they do" . . . The quotes go on and on. They all have merit and are based on logic. Much has been written in support of the premise that forgiveness denotes strength of character. It is two dimensional. One facet is the person requesting forgiveness. The other is the person from whom forgiveness is being sought.

Listening to literally hundreds of conversations in my home as well as when visiting my grandparents, I heard many conversations where the subject of forgiveness was discussed. Generally speaking, it was a very rare and unusual situation where perceived transgressions were not forgiven. In the Judaic faith, the most holy day of the year is Yom Kippur. This is the Day of Atonement. On this day, we ask forgiveness for all the sins we have committed before G-d (Leviticus 16:30). It is our belief that if we have sinned against another human being, forgiveness can only be granted by the person whom we mistreated. For all other violations, our plea for forgiveness is directed to G-d.

I have learned that asking for forgiveness is far more difficult than granting it. As a child, I was taught that whenever I did something wrong, I needed to apologize—for example, breaking into a line and not waiting my turn, saying something that resulted in hurt feelings, or generally misbehaving. A simple apology was insufficient. I had to admit to the wrongdoing without any excuse. To admit guilt is never easy due to all the explanations that were required. With questions such as "Why did you do that? Did you not know your actions were wrong? What were you thinking?" the interrogation seemed endless.

The punishment phase came next. Besides being asked to apologize and give a solemn oath there would be no recurrence, there would be a price to pay. The entire experience taught me that staying out of trouble would avoid the pain and strain.

It was quite easy to grant forgiveness. A simple "that's okay, I understand" or "all right, but don't do it again" was all that was needed and life went on.

As an adult, I look at forgiveness through two prisms. The first prism would include those actions we perceive to be harmful to ourselves or others we care about that are accidental and unintentional—for example, a car backing into another automobile, someone inadvertently breaking a fine piece of china, or a person missing a significant event without reason after accepting the invitation. These things happen. Accidents are part of life. Being inconsiderate is rude and poor behavior. The second prism refers to individuals who, with malice and forethought, commit actions such as lying, cheating, stealing, or slandering. In many cases, these result in permanent damage to another party. Besides having an adverse impact on reputations, they can also bring about physical, emotional, and financial consequences.

When accidents, oversights, and mistakes happen, they are upsetting, but the frustration is temporary, and I have learned to deal with it. Accept an apology should one be forthcoming, consider it part of life, and get over it. In the event someone intentionally causes distress, harm, or damage in any form to myself, a family member, someone dear to me, or a defenseless person, animal, or group of people that I do not know, I cannot and do not forgive. Moreover, I am unwilling to remain passive, and respond in an appropriate but lawful manner. This may include a range of actions such as letters, phone calls, or personal confrontation. Making my position and response clear serves as a great catharsis. This flaw in my personality does create some frustration with both Jody and other family members. Fortunately, with some reluctance, they do forgive and accept.

While I do believe I have strength of character, my behavior does contradict what many others have written about forgiveness representing strength of character. My rationalization is it does provide me with material to atone for on Yom Kippur. Over time, people have experienced situations that have been sources of anger, frustration, irritation, and even humiliation. For the most part during our formative years, we are taught that to forgive is proper and mature behavior. Human nature being what it is at times makes forgiveness difficult. It is one thing if something occurs by accident—someone stepping on our foot, being tardy, or using inappropriate language are some examples. More serious transgressions might include a vehicle accident, being slandered, or deception involving a monetary transaction. It is a natural reaction to become angry, respond with inappropriate comments, or even initiate a physical altercation. Overreacting can result in unintended consequences. By showing forgiveness, you can not only minimize long-term damage to a relationship, but also achieve inner peace by showing understanding and compassion. It may very well relieve stress and conserve our energy for more productive activities. To harbor anger or seek revenge serves no purpose other than to reinforce our anger. Without forgiveness, we very well can regress into a state of bitterness and perpetual anger. This may lead to an escalation of events resulting in adverse consequences.

On a personal note, I find forgiveness difficult to offer in certain situations. I have no problem in forgiving accidents, mistakes, or intellectual deficiency. I have great difficulty in offering forgiveness to someone who with malice and forethought is dishonest, deceptive, or disrespectful to me, someone, or something I care deeply about—be it my family, a friend, my country, religion, or employer.

Value Learned: Forgiveness is not always easy to do. It is a preferred trait over more negative reactions. However, it can be selective and used with discretion.

FRIENDSHIP

Friendship is a two-way street
It is priceless relationship that can't be beat

Friends come in all sizes, shapes, colors, genders, religions, political ideologies, and many other distinguishing characteristics. As we travel along the highway of life, we meet countless numbers of people. Some, we rarely if ever see again, and others become part of our life. Friendship is a very complex relationship due to the fact that it is influenced by a multitude of factors that include time, location, and situational change. There are an unlimited number of other circumstances that can impact friendship.

My first recollection of a friend was at the age of five. A boy in my first grade class asked if I would come to his birthday party. His mother called my mother, and I attended the party, brought a gift, played games, sang "Happy Birthday," and enjoyed the cake and ice cream. Our friendship endured through our school years. He was my best man at our wedding, as I was at his. Our careers took us to different cities, but we stayed in close communication for over seventy years. Unfortunately, his health deteriorated, and he was confined to an assisted living facility which precluded him from traveling. I continued to talk with him, and Jody and I would make the effort to travel and visit him when we were in that part of the country. Sadly, he passed away this past year, and I think of him often. Our friendship will always have great meaning and value to me. I have another friend that I met when I was seven. He too lives in another city. We visit periodically and exchange phone calls. We still call one another on our birthdays. True friends are forever.

To this day, I maintain contact with friendships made in college, the military, IBM, former neighbors, post-retirement, current business partners, and people we have met during our travels. The greatest teacher I ever had to instill the value of friendship is my dear wife. Jody has taken communicating with friends to a new level. True friendship is an ongoing relationship and not a temporary encounter.

Jody and me and our two best friends

I compare friendship to a landscape. Seeds, bulbs, shrubs, and trees can all be planted. Some take root and mature to tall, stately trees, healthy plants, beautiful flowers, and attractive ground cover. Proper care, water, nutrients, and sunshine made that possible. Another landscape without attention will soon wither and die. The lesson to be learned is that for friendship to mature and blossom, it needs attention and reinforcement. It cannot be taken for granted and revived when only one party needs some attention.

The question may be asked, "What constitutes friendship?" What I have learned is that some of the major components consist of:

- Trust—Someone will do what he or she says he or she will do.
- Integrity—Someone will act with honesty and sincerity.
- Sharing—A relationship that is not one-sided, but both give and take.
- Candor—Someone that will provide unfiltered advice and counsel and "tell it the way it is."
- Confidant—Shared private matters remain private.
- Supportive—Decisions agreed to will be supported when challenged.
- Intelligence—Someone who will promote intellectual, social, and spiritual growth.
- Loyalty—The belief that firm allegiance to one another exists.
- Humor—Everyone needs to smile once in a while.
- Dependable—When a need does require a call for assistance, the request will be answered immediately without reservation, questions, or indifference.

These represent my personal "Ten Commandments" of friendship. By no means are they all inclusive. Rather, they represent my own personal matrix based on what I have experienced interacting with many people for many years.

Over the years, I have concluded there are gradations when describing friendship. We can be "friendly" with people with whom we interact without being friends—for example, the cashier where we shop, the mail carrier, and the bank teller are familiar to us. While we may know them by name, we usually have no other interaction with them. The next level may include neighbors, people we work with, or congregants at our place of worship. The next category could very well include those individuals we choose to socialize with or go to dinner, a movie, or sporting event with. The next group could be those we enjoy traveling with, frequently communicate with, and be involved in significant family celebrations. Ultimately, we reach a level of "near and dear" friendship. This group consists of people who typically are included in all our activities. Finally, one or two individuals reach the level of "Best Friend." This person has reached the highest position of trust and confidence. This is the person that would receive our request for assistance if we had to make one phone call for help. This is also the person for whom we would go to any length to offer support and assistance. In summary, friendship is built on a foundation of trust, confidence, mutual interests in helping one another, and respect. This relationship is built over time, one block at a time. Friends may not always agree, but they understand and are faithful and loyal to one another.

Finally, before leaving this most important value, it is important that I include our nonhuman "Best Friends." Be they canine or feline, reptile or rodent, fish or fowl, somewhere along our journey we encounter G-d's creatures. The experience of caring for a pet is like no other. Returning home after a stressful day and being greeted by your dog is a unique experience. A cat may have a different approach, but even while appearing aloof, shows his or her love in his or her own way. We care for them and they become members of the family. When the day comes and they leave, the memories are cherished. The pain will subside; the wound will heal, but the scar remains. They are remembered. Our family has our personal cat memorial park on our property. Each grave has a floral arrangement changed in the fall and spring. It is illuminated in the evening. On the anniversary of their passing, the family gathers and recalls particular characteristics which endeared them to us.

Value Learned: Friends are forever.

My best man, my best friend

Honesty

Being trustworthy and fair
Is a wonderful pair

My mom usually took me with her when she went shopping. I really enjoyed being with her, and she loved walking with me and holding my hand. In retrospect, she really didn't have anyone to leave me with, so it worked out well all around.

The big trip of the week was a journey to downtown Minneapolis by streetcar. I loved sitting near the conductor and watching him collect the fares and drive the car. It was a special treat to go downtown on Saturday morning. Mom would shop and as a special treat take me to lunch at a Chinese restaurant before we returned home. The highlight of the entire experience was a visit to the premier Minneapolis department store named Dayton's. This was the forerunner to Dayton Hudson, which subsequently became Target.

The experience that occurred on one of these visits to Dayton's clearly will never be forgotten. While walking through one of the aisles holding hands, I noticed a ten-dollar bill lying on the floor. I quickly picked it up and put it in my pocket. Mom did see me pick something up but did not see what it was. She asked me what I had put in my pocket, and I told her it was some money and showed her the ten-dollar bill.

She asked, "What are you going to do with the ten dollars you found?"

Without much hesitation, I said, "I'm going to buy a new baseball glove."

The one my friend had cost eight dollars. It was more money than I could imagine, so I would have the glove and I could also buy some candy and a pack of baseball cards. I was very excited about my good fortune.

My joy quickly disappeared when Mom said she would like to talk with me and walked over to a nearby bench, where we discussed the entire event. She began the conversation with some questions. "Herschel, how do you think the ten-dollar bill got on the floor? Do you think it belonged to someone? While you are happy, do you think the person will be sad? Do you think the owner needed that money for something very important such as food, medicine, gasoline, or a present for someone?

My response was, "Finders keepers!" Seeing the look on her face, I quickly realized that was not the right answer and we would spend some more time on that bench discussing the matter.

She then took me through a number of simple but real alternative choices.

We could put the money back on the floor where I found it.

We could look around and see if someone was looking for something.

We could keep the money. (I liked that one.)

We could take it home, call the store manager, and ask if someone was looking for some money.

We could return the money to the store manager for safekeeping and await someone to claim it.

We had some discussion, and as I recall, I did little talking and mostly a lot of listening. We approached the department manager, and my mom asked me if I had something to tell the manager. With a little coaxing, I explained what happened. The manager was smiling and said he would put the ten-dollar bill in an envelope and keep it in the cash register for thirty days. He then said if no one claimed it within the thirty days, he would call our house and tell me to come to the store, and he would then give me the money.

I was not overly excited about the plan, but understood it was the "right" thing to do. Mom then told me that sometimes the right thing to do is not always the easiest thing to do. If the owner did claim the money, I should feel good that I made that person happy. If the money was not claimed, I should feel good that I made the effort to help and for that effort, a reward was earned, but more importantly, I did something that was right.

Finally, my mom said, "I know you wanted a new baseball glove, but trust me—the glove will someday wear out, but the feeling of doing the right thing will always be with you."

Waiting for the thirty days to pass seemed like forever. Even though the manager said I should call him after thirty days, there was no way I could wait. I called him every day when I came home from school. I called him on Saturday afternoon. He was very patient and chuckled as he said, "No one asked about the money, Herschel. Sleep well and do well in school. Talk to you tomorrow."

The big day finally arrived. I called the manager, who by now had become my close friend and was absolutely elated when he said, "Herschel, the ten dollars now belongs to you. Have your mom bring you into the store and I will hand you the money."

Off we went to the store. It seemed forever until the streetcar arrived downtown. I ran up to the manager, and he was all smiles and had two other people with him. He told the others the entire story and gave me the envelope with the ten-dollar bill. The manager and the two others clapped, and my mom started to cry. I could hardly wait to leave and buy the baseball glove I so badly wanted. However, there was one more thing the manager wanted to say. He held my hand and said, "Herschel, you are an honest little boy, and I want you to know that when you grow up, if you ever want to work for the Dayton company, you tell your story about the ten dollars and you will have a job with us."

As the years passed I was fortunate enough to find other objects and I tried my best to facilitate finding the owner of the lost objects. Sometimes it was as easy as just picking something up after seeing the owner dropping the item and being unaware of the loss. Other times, it was trying to find the rightful owner.

In any event, whenever the situation does arise, I can't help thinking back to my experience at the Dayton department store.

Value Learned: Honesty reflects on you as a person. It may not always be easy to do, but the rewards are a clear conscience and knowing in your heart you did the right thing.

My Cub Scout card

Humor

Humor is something that creates a smile
It relieves stress and doesn't go out of style

As we look back on our life, we all can recall situations that we found to be humorous—for example, arriving at a party on the wrong date and time and being greeted by a very surprised host, realizing you left your wallet at home when the restaurant check was presented, or locking your keys in the car when you were trying to impress your first date and having to call for assistance. In retrospect, the often-used phrase "Things happen!" certainly is applicable to these incidents. We can easily learn to double-check our appointment calendar, ensure we have sufficient funds prior to leaving home, and have a spare automobile key available. I have personally experienced each of these embarrassing situations. Every one served as a learning experience. I now have a magnetic key holder on my automobile containing both a car and house key. I formed a habit of checking the next-day appointment calendar each evening prior to retiring. Finally, with the advanced technology currently available, my phone provides access to funds.

At times, however, "Things happen!" which are not at all humorous and become quite disturbing. The ability to endure these experiences, and upon reflection accept them as part of life, can also be quite stressful. When appropriate, finding some humor in these situations can be an invaluable lesson. I try to not get angry with myself and instead take the situation lightly. Comments such as "I guess age is catching up with me," or "At least I still remember my name" take off some of the edge.

There are good days and some that are not-so-good. There are days when nothing seems to go right. That's called life. We sometimes say to ourselves, "What else can go wrong?" And then something does. It's just one of those days. Hopefully we can look forward to tomorrow and believe it will be better than today. It may not always be easy to smile, but we must maintain a confident outlook that "this too shall pass." I have selected three experiences that serve as lessons illustrating how laughter can overcome stress.

My sister Harriet, who now
claims to be my younger sister

THE HONEYMOON

In the months before our wedding, Jody suggested that since we had the entire summer before we had to relocate from Chicago to Ft. Lee, Virginia, a nice relaxing automobile trip to the Pacific Northwest to include Lake Louise and Banff, Canada, would be a great honeymoon. Not wanting to start the marriage with any sign of disagreement, I readily agreed. About two weeks before the wedding, Jody had a change of mind, and the new plan was rather than travel to Canada, we would travel to Acapulco, Mexico, still by automobile. When I commented that this was 1956, the interstate highway system in the United States was under construction, and the roads in Mexico were questionable at best, my sense of adventure was questioned. The journey began June 26, 1956. We traveled south through states we had never seen.

All was going well until we encountered our first of many challenges. We were driving near Vicksburg, Mississippi, and we came upon some local citizens dressed in antebellum costumes celebrating along the road. They waved us over to stop and approached our car. Knowing that our automobile had Minnesota license plates and we were now in the Deep South, we had visions of a reenactment of a Civil War battle. The stress was quickly relieved when they offered us lemonade and cookies. We laughed and never forgot the experience.

As the trip progressed, there were a number of other contentious situations that arose that, in retrospect, were very insignificant. We did not agree on where to stop to eat, what kind of food, how many miles to drive, things about the wedding, and on and on. We both had private thoughts on whether this marriage was even going to last through the trip. I could only think that there was a return trip home ahead of me. When we arrived at the Mexican border, we had no papers to enter Mexico, and that caused another discussion as to who was responsible for getting the proper documents. When we solved that obstacle, we blamed each other for misreading the map and as a result getting lost. There were other issues, and by the time we arrived at our destination, we were barely speaking and Jody hurled her wedding rings into the ocean. Luckily, I was able to retrieve them, and we looked at each other and started to laugh. We agreed then and there to not let little clouds cover the blue sky and sun. The next sixty years were absolutely wonderful. Whenever an issue occurred, we talked and eventually laughed and moved on. Jody has been able to tolerate most of my many liabilities, and to her, I am forever grateful.

RUSSIA

The year was 1995. I decided to do something to help others and offered my services as a volunteer to the International Executive Service Corp. The organization was appreciative and assigned me to assist a young Russian entrepreneur in St. Petersburg, Russia. This gentleman had started a small computer distribution business. Having never been to Russia, I viewed this as a most interesting opportunity. The only reference in my mind was how my dad described the country when he was a young man and his recollection of Czar Nicholas II. I requested and it was agreed that Jody would accompany me on this adventure. The challenge awaiting us was a three-month assignment in Russia during the coldest winter months. I made arrangements for the journey and off we went, leaving on January 30, 1995.

A major issue arose when we arrived in St. Petersburg on January 31 and our visas were not valid until February 1. The Russian officials were not too understanding of our dilemma and took the position of denying us entry. After some negotiation and exchange of some US currency, the problem went away. My spouse was not too pleased with my visa application process, which created the problem and expressed her position very clearly. The next issue surfaced when we were not met and had to find transportation and a hotel. I set out in the airport for assistance and was on the phone when I felt something pressing against my back. I turned around and standing behind me was a Russian soldier with his rifle at my back. He was ordering me out of the airport. As I was leaving, I saw Jody also leaving, and we learned there was a bomb threat that forced an evacuation. The next scenario was the two of us, with our luggage, standing outside the airport in the cold and snow and no place to go. Words cannot do justice to the comments that my dear wife sent my way. We finally got a taxi to take us to a hotel. To summarize, it was a perfect description of a cold and silent night.

The next morning, we awoke and recalled the events of the previous evening. We began to laugh and said to each other, "Who would ever believe this story?" My frustration with Jody's lack of understanding of my error and her complete frustration with my incompetence in handling travel arrangements evaporated with some laughter, and our journey continued.

The entire Russian visit that started with incredible stress evolved into one of our most interesting and personally rewarding experiences. I had the satisfaction of helping the young man in his business, and Jody taught English to some Russian children.

We maintained our relationship with our Russian friends over the years. In 2012, we returned to Russia as tourists. This time, our documents were in order. We were greatly impressed with the progress of their company, and we laughed together with them about our initial trip to Russia. The entire adventure will forever be one of our most humorous experiences. Humor truly is a great prescription for stress relief.

THE KIMONO

In 1986, Jody and I decided to visit Japan. One of the highlights was a visit to a beautiful location named Hakone. This location was noted for its natural beauty, and it was famous for hot springs.

We had reservations at a beautiful hotel and were given a most impressive room. Besides a great view, it also featured a large hot tub. After the long trip, Jody decided to relax in the hot tub. I was trying to rest and was without clothes when there was a knock at the door. Simultaneously with the knock, a woman entered the room, carrying a kimono. I later learned that the custom at this hotel was for evening dinner, all men were to wear a ceremonial kimono. She was there to present me with the kimono I was to wear at dinner that evening.

Jody, who was relaxing in the hot tub, also with no clothes, was more than a little upset with the lady having zero respect for a guest's privacy. The lady clearly was not the least bit concerned and was intent on putting the kimono on me to see if it fit properly and instructing me on how to tie it correctly. Not being used to all this attention, I grabbed the bedspread in an attempt at modesty. This effort was of no avail as the lady was intent on accomplishing her mission and took the bedspread from me.

With her assignment completed, she thanked me, smiled, and left. The initial reaction Jody and I had was one of anger and upset over the disrespect for privacy. We were venting our emotions when suddenly we started to laugh. We realized the cultural divide and started to look at each other. The visual had to be hilarious— Jody in the hot tub, and me standing there in a very loose-fitting kimono. We burst into laughter and chalked it up to another story to someday share with children and grandchildren. Just another example where stress was melted with humor.

Value Learned: Maintain a positive attitude, "After every storm, the sun will once again reappear."

Another photo with my "younger sister"

INTEGRITY

Integrity is being honest and sincere
It is something to be held very dear

One of the most valuable assets one can possess is integrity. When we say or promise something to someone, we have pledged our reputation. If we deliver whatever we proclaimed, trust is gained and our word is deemed to be "golden." In the event the opposite occurs, trust and confidence can be significantly diminished. Lack of or diminishing integrity will have a severe impact on the ability of a person to succeed in any endeavor. The one thing you need to learn early in life is the value of your word. It is both a valuable and highly perishable commodity. It takes time, energy, and experience to gain and can be destroyed in a single event taking but a brief moment. Once lost, it is extremely difficult to regain. Whether it is a financial or contractual transaction, a verbal promise, or merely a conversation, people rely on your integrity. Second chances are difficult to come by.

I never realized until later in life that my first experience with integrity began on November 20, 1944. I was ten, and on that date, I signed my Cub Card. One of the stipulations of becoming a Cub Scout was "I PROMISE to do my best." I really did not understand the meaning of the word "promise." It however became one of the basic precepts that have governed my behavior.

As a teenager, it was always interesting to listen to my dad and my maternal grandfather share some of their practical experiences. In retrospect, many of these conversations concerned integrity.

However, that was not the label that was used by them. It was only in later life did I realize what they were unknowingly teaching me.

I remember my dad talking about a situation involving a friend that purchased an apartment building in the 1920s. He asked my dad to loan him some money to facilitate the transaction. When the Great Depression occurred in the early 1930s, the friend could no longer maintain the mortgage on the property, let alone repay my dad for his loan. Dad told his friend that he would personally continue to make the mortgage payments to protect the investment. At some significant sacrifice, my dad did make every payment as promised, thereby protecting his friend's investment. Dad was very proud of his action and stressed the importance of keeping a promise once made.

My grandfather was not wealthy. He worked very hard in his business but never accumulated any significant financial assets. He had a deep belief in helping those in need, as well as contributing to multiple charitable causes, and did what he could, however small the amount. On many occasions, he speculated if ever he had more resources he would like to share them with others. His fortunes did turn in the early 1950s. The land upon which his business was located was deemed prime real estate for development. The result enabled him to fulfill his ultimate dream. He, too, like my dad, was most proud of keeping his word.

These gentlemen never used the word "integrity," though they did say over and over, "If your word is worthless, you have nothing." They continued with, "Once lost, your word cannot be repurchased."

Those were important values and have served me well in both my personal and professional life. It is easy to make a promise. On occasion, it may be difficult to fulfill the promise. One real but somewhat humorous challenge I faced involved a dear uncle of mine. He had a most interesting life, and on his eighty-fifth birthday, I asked him to please write his memoirs for the benefit of the family. One of his favorite pastimes was fishing. He promised to write his memoir if I would promise to go ice fishing with him. I readily agreed and gave my word to accompany him on an ice fishing trip. Given his age, I was confident that event would not materialize. I was very surprised when he called and invited me to accompany him on the trip he had arranged. I initially declined until he reminded me of my promise. The result was I left Atlanta on a nice sunny day and the next day found myself in a cabin on the shore of Lake of the Woods in Canada. The actual temperature was minus forty degrees Fahrenheit. The trip was only three days, although it seemed like three months. I returned to Atlanta with three fish and a cold. I calculated the cost of keeping this promise at approximately nine hundred dollars. However, my uncle believed my integrity was intact. That alone made the entire experience worthwhile.

On a more serious note, over the course of my lifetime, there have been innumerable times when I made promises that obligated me to some action — whether they involved being at a certain place at a certain time, providing advice and counsel when called upon by a friend, delivering on assistance that I had promised, helping in a volunteer activity, serving a nonprofit organization, or whatever other opportunity has come my way. When we say, "Call me if I can ever be of help," one must take that seriously and literally. Otherwise don't say it.

Integrity is under constant challenge from external pressures. A prime example is the political arena. During a political campaign, candidates articulate many promises. Once elected, the promises made may very well be replaced with excuses why they were not kept. Another example is many advertisements contain "half-truths." Once something is purchased, only then we may learn of disclaimers or conditions that were omitted or hidden in mice type with the hope they would not be discovered. Conversely, we have learned that certain manufacturers and merchants can be relied upon to fulfill their promises. These are organizations that we continue to interact with due to the reputation they have earned through their integrity.

The lesson I have learned is people count on our word. Integrity, like trust, is fragile and perishable. It takes time and effort to achieve. One event can destroy what required years to acquire. For integrity to endure, it cannot be selective. It must be reinforced with every opportunity one is presented with.

Value Learned: Integrity is perishable—protect it at all costs.

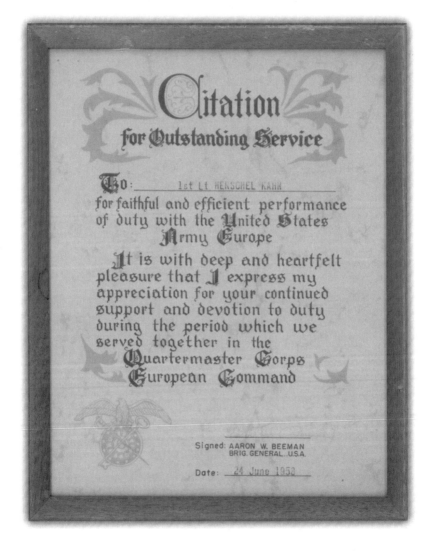

Army citation for outstanding service

LOVE

Love is unconditional and should grow each day
Its foundation is pleasing someone in every way

Rarely a day passes without hearing the word "love." It is very common to describe an inanimate subject such as food, clothing, automobile, jewelry or a host of other items with the phrase "I love it." The same holds true of our appreciation of events. We exclaim our love for movies, trips, classes, sermons, parties, or plays, to name just a few. While these items and events may very well be deserving of the love accolade, they pale in importance when compared to describing a personal relationship.

The memory of an outstanding dinner fades with time. The automobile that once was the centerpiece attraction ages and eventually is disposed of. Clothing at some point finds its way to thrift shops, and jewelry is most likely bequeathed to the next generation. Events, too, fade with time. It is difficult to remember which movies were nominated for awards this year, let alone try to recall what was the best motion picture five years ago. We leave our house of worship extolling the sermon just preached. However, trying to recall the message sent a month ago might present a challenge.

My mother taught me a lesson about love that I shall always remember. When I misbehaved, she was not at all shy about letting me know how she felt. When she finished expressing her disappointment or anger, I would ask her a question: "Mom, do you still like me?"

Her answer more often than not was, "I don't like the way you behaved, but I will always love you."

I asked what the difference was, and her answer was, "Sometimes I like what you did, sometimes I don't like what you did, but I will always love you."

I asked again what the difference was. She answered, "Liking something comes and goes, but love is forever."

To cover all bases, I then developed a special question: "Do you like and love me?"

Jody and I, 1954

Over the years, I have thought about her definition of love many times. Without realizing it, I'm sure she meant that loving someone is deeper and more permanent than liking someone.

As time passed and maturity took hold, I gave considerable thought to what love actually meant to me. It became far more important than describing how much I liked things, events, or experiences. Rather, it defined my feelings about people with whom I interacted. I began to understand that love was closely tied to commitment. The phrase "I would do anything for that individual" took on a real meaning. The feeling we have for our parents, spouses, and children exemplifies the true meaning of love. We are committed to caring and assisting them to our fullest capability. Love supersedes other emotions such as anger or disappointment. It is total commitment to helping and understanding someone regardless of the situation.

Love is also reflected in causes that we embrace—for example, love of country. This love resides in our belief that our country is unlike any other country. We believe it offers opportunity, freedom, and a quality of life that makes it unique. We love our religion as it embodies and fulfills our faith-based needs whatever they may be. We love our family and are committed to the caring, helping, and protecting each member.

I believe that love is also intuitive. The first time we hold our newborn, the feeling of love for that precious, innocent little life overwhelms us. When the euphoria of the event diminishes and we realize what the road ahead entails, our love gives us the strength to provide all within our power to nurture and protect that child regardless of what sacrifice it may require. As we watch parents age and become less self-sufficient, we willingly assume the responsibility for their care and comfort.

I reflect on some difficult moments in my professional and personal life when things for a variety of reasons were not going well. Jody was always there to provide the love, support, and patience needed to guide me. Together over our long marriage, we have experienced some difficult times, and it was our love for each other that leveled both mountains and valleys. That to me was true love in action. It is easy to say, "I love you," but it is real love when you can prove it.

Poems have been written, books have been published, and songs have been composed about it. but true love comes from within. It is a deep, honest, emotional feeling that sincerely communicates our innermost feelings. Many people over many years have taught me the value of love. My dear wife and premier teacher reminds me often how much she loves me, and then adds (hopefully in jest), "Who else would put up with you?"

Value Learned: Love is mutual. It embodies caring, sharing, compromising, and respect. It is timeless.

My parents and Jody, 1955

LOYALTY

Loyalty can't be purchased; it comes from the heart
It endures whether we are together or far apart

I remember a conversation my parents were having at dinner one evening. The subject they were discussing related to a small grocery store located close to our home. My mother was telling my dad that a large supermarket was going to open a facility also nearby. It did not surprise them that prices at the large chain store would be less than the corner grocery. They quickly agreed to continue shopping at the small store versus the supermarket. I asked why they decided not to change and pay less. They proceeded to give me my first lesson concerning loyalty. They knew the owner of the small store and his wife.

While they were not close friends, they did have a friendship that was built on years of shopping at that store. My dad explained further that in the event people did not continue buying groceries at the corner grocery, it would soon have to go out of business. If saving a few dollars would harm the small business, my dad said it would not be the right thing to do. He further went on to say, "It just isn't worth it." He did not use the word "loyalty," but in retrospect it was my first lesson involving that value. Later in life, I realized what he was teaching me was that loyalty is not built on price. It is built on relationships. To this day, we continually receive solicitations to change banks, insurance brokers, automobile service centers, home service providers, and many other assorted merchants. The primary enticement usually is price. Loyalty for us still prevails.

Throughout life, we are exposed to situations and events that reinforce a sense of allegiance and dedication to a belief. As a child in grade school, it was a daily occurrence to start the day with the pledge of allegiance to our country. It troubles me greatly that in some venues today, this practice has been discontinued. I attended North High School in Minneapolis. The school song began with the phrase, "We're loyal to you, North Side High." Upon graduating college and completing ROTC training, I took a loyalty oath prior to receiving a commission as a military officer.

Numerous family members served in the military, and as a result, a deep sense of loyalty to our country was passed to me. At times my loyalty has been tested. One such example occurred during an overseas trip. During a tour, some individuals were making some disparaging remarks about our country. After listening for about five minutes, I responded in a less than tactful way, and it became quite clear to them where my loyalty was positioned. Some of the remarks which I took exception to included "Americans are arrogant and self-centered" and "Americans flaunt their wealth and look down upon Europeans."

The remarks were not made in subdued tones, but at a level that was purposely made for my benefit. My response was polite but firm. I said that "I could not help overhearing your remarks, and I take great exception to your comments. My country has been more than generous to all European countries in the form of both blood and treasure. For you not to appreciate what America has done, I find insulting and I suggest you be quiet." The interaction ceased at that point. They understood my emotional response. I believe individuals have every right to level criticism about any subject they choose. However, the criticism is not immune from a response be it based on loyalty, facts, or a difference of opinion.

Loyalty is a key component to the structure that forms our lifestyle. The clergy play a role in our religious loyalty. Management can have a significant impact on how we view our employer. The interaction we have with our friends serves to form loyal relationships. The phrase "through thick and thin" often defines friendship.

My parents and grandparents were great teachers about the value of family loyalty. Over the years, I witnessed countless examples of the family coming to the aid of another member in need. My dad took it upon himself to insure his parents' and siblings' needs were met. Jody's family also prioritized assisting one another to insure all were cared for.

Loyalty is boundless. In one form or another, it exists across all cultures. It is not limited to humans. I marvel at the animal kingdom. What an incredible experience to come home after a long day and be greeted immediately by the household pet. We observe examples of various animals and birds that care for each other in time of need. Whether it is instinctive or learned, it does exist.

It is easy to profess loyalty. However, at times our commitment to this value can be challenging. The moment of truth occurs when we have an opportunity to speak up in support of our beliefs. Another example would be coming to the aid of a friend that is being attacked, either physically or verbally. Loyalty requires both dedication and devotion. It is not something to be turned on and off. This value can be very challenging. Providing candid and justified criticism to a friend is an act of loyalty, although it may not be received positively. Likewise, being the recipient of candor needs to be looked upon as an act of loyalty. I have learned over time this value requires a long-term commitment. It is not selective and is perishable if not used consistently. It is not a convenience item. When difficult situations arise and we look for help, loyalty will be quickly identified.

Value Learned: Defend your position, remain loyal to your cause, but recognize dissent and criticism also have to be endured.

MANAGEMENT

Management is getting things done through people
Respect, candor, and sensitivity make it simple

One definition of management is "to direct or control the behavior or movement of people." While I did have some management courses in college, I had absolutely no practical experience. My first management opportunity occurred when I was in the military service. Having taken ROTC at the University of Minnesota, I entered the army with the rank of second lieutenant. Upon completion of basic school at Ft. Lee, Virginia, I was given the assignment of commissary officer at a base in Rochefort, France. Suddenly I found myself in charge of fifteen soldiers, together with about ten French civilian employees. In addition, I became responsible for US government property having a value of approximately three million dollars.

Adding to the insecurity of this twenty-three-year-old lieutenant was the fact that I never managed anything or anyone, didn't understand the job, and didn't speak French.

The good thing was I knew what I did not know. Knowing that I needed help, I approached an "old" — he was probably in his late thirties, but to me he was old — master sergeant in my organization. I told him of my concerns and asked for his help. He was surprised and somewhat appreciative of the opportunity. His help was invaluable. He willingly shared his knowledge and experience and guided me through what could have been a most difficult situation. Reflecting on this experience, the lesson I learned was that when you don't know something, ask for help and guidance. As a result of teaming with the sergeant, at the conclusion of the assignment, we were awarded an outstanding citation from the commanding general.

LESSON ONE—KNOW WHAT YOU DON'T KNOW!

After completing my military service, I returned to Chicago and was fortunate to be hired by the IBM Corporation in 1959. I began my career in an entry-level position as one of many administrative employees having the responsibility of processing paperwork.

One day, my manager arranged a meeting together with his manager to talk to me about my performance. This was unusual and not a good sign. The meeting began with my manager saying, "Herschel, of all the administrative employees we have in this department, you are the least productive person we have." At this point, I was thinking how I was going to tell my dear wife that I had been fired. The manager then went on to say that my work was very accurate; however, my productivity was unacceptable. Before I could offer anything in my defense, he then continued, "Given the situation, we have decided to promote you to a management position." The reason provided was that although my performance was unsatisfactory, people seemed to like me and I appeared to work well with others. The next comment was "Managers don't have to know much; they just need to get the work done through others." So began what was a long, fulfilling, and satisfying management career with a world-class organization. While the definition of management given was over-simplified, it did define one key component—the ability to relate to others.

LESSON TWO—STRONG INTERPERSONAL SKILLS

It was a privilege to work with many exceptional managers throughout my career. Each one, in his or her way, taught me the art of managing. Their styles may have been different. However, the fundamental values they possessed were the threads that formed the fabric of an exemplary management mosaic.

My bias has always been and remains that the key to management success is building a strong team. Lead by example, delegate, develop, listen, take responsibility, respect others, be decisive, and be organized are but a few traits that are essential ingredients for a successful management recipe. It would be redundant to elaborate on these characteristics, given that volumes have been written about the subject. Indeed, there are other values that will be discussed as the learning process continues.

Value Learned: Management is an art requiring ability to achieve goals through people. It requires leadership, delegation, listening, organizational, and people skills.

First IBM check, November 1959

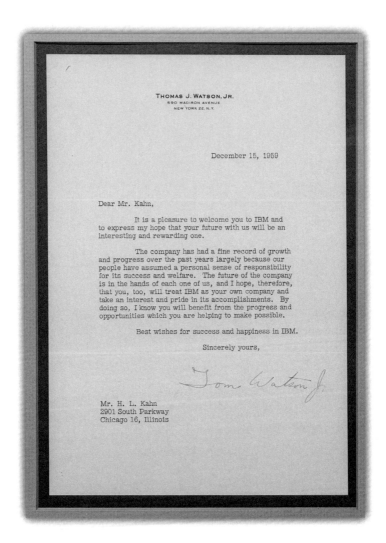

THOMAS J. WATSON, JR.
590 MADISON AVENUE
NEW YORK 22, N.Y.

December 15, 1959

Dear Mr. Kahn,

It is a pleasure to welcome you to IBM and to express my hope that your future with us will be an interesting and rewarding one.

The company has had a fine record of growth and progress over the past years largely because our people have assumed a personal sense of responsibility for its success and welfare. The future of the company is in the hands of each one of us, and I hope, therefore, that you, too, will treat IBM as your own company and take an interest and pride in its accomplishments. By doing so, I know you will benefit from the progress and opportunities which you are helping to make possible.

Best wishes for success and happiness in IBM.

Sincerely yours,

Tom Watson Jr.

Mr. H. L. Kahn
2901 South Parkway
Chicago 16, Illinois

Welcome to IBM!

Marriage

We remember the wine, music, and cake
Do not forget the vows we did make

"For better, for worse," "In sickness and health," "Until death do us part." These vows are a high point of most wedding ceremonies. Unfortunately, all too often, they are not kept. Statistics commonly portray that half of all marriages in the United States end in divorce. From an introspective point of view, I certainly am not an expert on the subject. However, as I write, Jody and I are looking forward to our sixtieth wedding anniversary.

I have often thought about the subject as it relates to my family when I was a child. During that time period, divorce was frowned upon. Perhaps that had some impact, but I believe relationships start from a common agreement on specific values. I had cousins that were married for over sixty years. My parents and grandparents had long marriages; my sister and uncles also had long-lasting marriages. I do believe the environment I experienced did have an effect on how I viewed marriage as both a commitment as well as a relationship.

People have said to me, "You're lucky." I disagree with that categorization. Luck can come into play with the roll of the dice, the spin of a roulette wheel, being in the right place at the right time, or being in the wrong place at the wrong time. In my view, marriage requires two people working hard as a team to make it successful. It is not a function of luck.

Wedding photo, June 24, 1956

Reasons given for divorce are vague and don't really address the core issues. Irreconcilable differences, irretrievable breakdown of the marriage, or incompatibility are but a few examples. These words may very well satisfy legal requirements. The bigger question is, what transpired from the time both partners recited their marriage vows?

Life's journey provides literally thousands of opportunities for decision making. Without a doubt, the very best decision I ever made was to ask Jody to marry me.

We met in 1950 at a Hebrew-speaking camp located near Conover, Wisconsin. She lived in Chicago, and I resided in Minneapolis. We did not know each other previously, although my best friend had met her on a prior occasion and told me about her. It was a very unusual event that caused us to meet. I was playing in a basketball game. During the game, the ball went off the court into a group of campers. Jody happened to catch the ball and threw it back on the court. There was one small problem—I was concentrating on playing and when she threw the ball it struck me and broke my glasses. Needless to say, I was more than a little upset, turned to the group watching and asked, "What fool would throw a ball when a player wasn't looking?" This little attractive blonde raised her hand and waved at me. The rest is history. It does reinforce the belief that some things are just meant to happen.

Over the next several years, we communicated by letters, and when I could scrape up some extra money, I would place a long-distance call. She decided to attend the University of Minnesota for her junior and senior years, and there was no doubt in my mind how very special she was. We had a great deal in common, and when we disagreed on a few things, we would laugh and still maintain our views without becoming angry at each other. We became engaged at the end of our junior year and married one year later, June 24, 1956.

We talked about many things, but in retrospect, some of the major subjects that surfaced later in life were not discussed because neither of us had considered them. For example, raising children, a career that required travel and relocation, managing finances, and relationships with other family members were not a high priority. One thing that became very clear was that she absolutely did not want to live in Minneapolis. Even though that was my home and I never thought of leaving, that was not going to become an obstacle for me. The learning point being if you want something badly enough, you may have to give something in return.

Aside from a "rocky" honeymoon, which was discussed earlier, the journey has been absolutely wonderful. I can honestly say that there has never been what can be described as a major argument. Some of my antics, habits, and idiosyncrasies I am sure caused Jody consternation, but a few choice comments put things back on track.

The journey has been anything but boring. We have lived in six different homes, three countries, raised four children, brought our grandson to our home from a foreign country, traveled the world, met hundreds of people, maintained friendships across the globe, cared for innumerable pets, pursued our careers, and remain very much in love.

At our fiftieth wedding anniversary, we received the inevitable question, "To what do you attribute your long and successful marriage?" My answer was compromise. My reason for that answer was based on the belief that marriage is a partnership. There are times when both parties will not agree on a specific course of action. My view when dealing with an impasse is the belief that, "This too shall pass." One should not let a bump in the road ruin the rest of the trip. For the most part, Jody and I share this vision, which leads to mutual concession, and life goes on. When that strategic move fails, my backup plan is capitulation. It is less expensive than alimony.

Jody's answer to the same question was trust. Her thought was based on confidence that I would not do anything that would disappoint her, given my career entailed extensive travel. To do otherwise would, in her words, "Drive [her] to drink."

In retrospect, the fact that my parents had mutual respect for one another, arguments were minimal and short lived. and the home atmosphere was warm and friendly served as a lesson for what constitutes a good marriage. They were great teachers.

Value Learned: The two most critical values to a lasting, loving, and successful marriage are compromise and trust.

40 Years of Wedded Bliss

To the love of my life

It was a sunny June day in 1950 that I will never forget
It was our first day at Camp Ramah where you and I met

Six years later in Chicago we said "I do"
A half century has gone by and we still say "I love you!"

The journey has been filled with valleys and hills
Sadness and happiness and many great thrills

We have been blessed with four wonderful children and a grandson
A life of good health, great friends, world travel and lots of fun

You have kept us on course as you stood by my side
You will always be my beautiful loving bride

Thanks for each and every thing you do
You are the love of my life—I love you!

Herschel   June 24th, 2006

Poem I wrote to Jody for our
fiftieth wedding anniversary, June 24, 2006

Memories

Memories are a link to the past
They serve as a reminder how time goes so fast

As we take a trip back through time, we realize what a valuable tool our memory is. There are innumerable examples of experiences that I certainly did not appreciate at the time they were being taught.

To this very day, whenever I walk across a street, regardless if the traffic signal is green, I look in both directions to see if oncoming traffic will stop. Where did I learn that was a precaution one must practice? The genesis of this habit originated when, as a child, whenever my mother took me for a walk, she always held my hand. When we came to a crosswalk she would say, "Watch your sides." She would then explain, "You must first look to the left, then to the right, to ensure there was no traffic approaching." This statement, "watch your sides," was repeated over and over even as an adult. She was teaching me a fundamental act of safety. To this day as I walk across an intersection, I recall my mother's words.

Another lesson taught that at the time I didn't realize was a lesson related to tying my shoes. Often when I tie my shoes, the thought goes through my mind: *How and when did I learn this routine but very necessary act?* I remember that I had great difficulty learning how to tie my shoes. My sister had no patience to work with me, so my mother took up the task. I tried to take the easy way out by asking her each morning to tie my shoes. Her answer was always the same: "Someday, if I am not with you, who will tie your shoes? You had better learn now." Another lesson would then follow—her way of teaching self-reliance.

117

My boyhood home

Continuing, as a young boy, I was constantly cautioned about talking to strangers. In retrospect, the origin of this lesson was most interesting. Our home was a very short distance from the elementary school I attended. This made it very convenient for me to walk home for lunch, talk with my mom, and get back to school on time for my afternoon class.

At that point in time, this was a very common practice. One day as I was close to home, I saw a lady walking toward me wearing a very pretty white, decorated dress. She asked my name and where I was going. I told her my name and replied that I was going home for lunch. I asked her name and she told me hers. Then, I asked if she would like to come to my home and have lunch with me and my mother. She smiled and said that would be very nice.

What I did not know that about two city blocks from our house, there was a hospital for adults with what today would be diagnosed as dementia. The pretty white dress was the hospital gown. The decoration was the hospital logo. I brought my new friend into the house and introduced her to my mother. Mom immediately understood the situation, was very calm, and asked me to talk with the lady while she returned to the kitchen. Mom did go to another room and called the hospital to let them know we had a guest who perhaps they were missing.

Within minutes, two members of the hospital staff arrived to claim their missing person. The lady thanked me for my kindness and said she was sorry she could not stay for lunch. The lesson followed, and best that I remember it, was a compliment for being kind. However, it was also a very clear caution about talking to strangers. I fondly remember that experience. The irony of it is that in my professional life, I met and talked to hundreds of strangers. It became a natural and very comfortable part of my personality. However, I never again had the pleasure of walking and meeting an unattended hospital patient and inviting him or her to lunch.

The link between memories and learning becomes stronger with each event we recall. The list can become endless once we begin to think back to some of our experiences. Some events overshadow others, but in the aggregate, they all contribute to our reservoir of knowledge and hopefully wisdom. Take a moment and drift back in time:

- First day of school in kindergarten
- First religious experience
- Teachers you liked and disliked
- First pet
- First dollar you ever earned
- First date
- First dance
- High school
- First day of college
- First car
- Getting engaged
- First career position
- First promotion
- Getting married
- First house
- Meeting neighbors
- First time you held each of your newborn children

- Teaching your children how to ride a bike, fish, sports, cooking, sewing, and more
- First realizing your parents and grandparents did know a few things
- First trip away from home
- First funeral
- First day of retirement

Time passes ever so quickly, and as the pace increases, we typically do not take time to recall past events. However, these past events have had significant influence on the values we embrace. Take a moment to reflect on the values we cherish:

- The importance of getting along with others
- The importance of maintaining our property
- The importance of managing our finances
- The importance of education
- The importance of loving all of G-d's creatures
- The importance of dedication and commitment for career success
- The importance of respect, compromise, and love in marriage
- The importance of providing care, love, and guidance to our children
- The importance of knowing that those who came before us did know something
- The importance of offering assistance to others
- The importance of understanding no one is eternal, embrace them when you can
- The importance and significance faith can have in our life
- The words of a very great song, "Thanks for the Memories," tell it all

Value Learned: Memories are the foundation of our past and the vision for our future.

ORGANIZATION

Attention to organization
Will greatly reduce frustration

Being organized means different things to different people. The term itself has very broad meaning. Some people would consider themselves to be organized if they know precisely where to look to find an item they are seeking. Someone else would consider him or herself organized when every item he or she owns is in a specific place and there is zero clutter to serve as a distraction. His or her living areas look neat as a pin. Another individual is proud of the fact that he or she prepares a shopping list prior to visiting the supermarket, thereby forgetting nothing. Other examples would include labeling keys, keeping an appointment calendar, filing important documents, or developing a system to remember key dates. The list of examples is endless. There are individuals that take great pride in organizing every phase of their lives. At times, they may even cross the line and try to organize the lives of others. That behavior provides excellent candidates for professional therapists specializing in conflict resolution.

My family was a study of organizational contrast. My grandfather was perhaps the most disorganized individual I ever knew. If awards were presented for least organized people, he would be selected for the all-star team. Without exception, anytime I visited his house, he and grandma would be having an animated disagreement about the location of a specific item or document.

Eventually whatever he was trying to find was located where he had misplaced it.

At the opposite end of the spectrum was one of his sons, a very dear uncle of mine. This gentleman was one of the most organized individuals I ever encountered. The contrast between father and son convinced me that organization is certainly not genetic.

My mother was the best teacher I had when it came to being organized. She went to great lengths to explain that organization has many facets. She stressed that time management was one of the most critical factors of being organized. She taught me that everything has a place and there needs to be a place for everything. Another lesson also related to time. She would show me how much time was wasted looking for lost items. She also taught me about prioritizing time. On a regular basis, she would reference both my grandfather and my uncle to make a particular point on the results of both good and bad organizational behavior.

Observing the behavior of others can serve as a valuable lesson as it applies to being organized. There are people that keep accurate and current material for tax purposes, while others bring whatever information they saved to their tax preparer in a shoebox. Some people decide to pack for a trip the day of their departure. These individuals invariably forget something they wish they had remembered. Another example is the person searching for an address or phone number versus the person that has all such information properly stored. Misplacing a document, forgetting an appointment, overlooking an important date such as a birthday or a friend's anniversary, or maybe that of your spouse, can all be more than slightly embarrassing.

I was fortunate to have parents that taught basic organizational concepts during my childhood years. It was understood my responsibilities consisted of keeping my room neat, hanging up clothes, and selecting what I was to wear the next day prior to going to sleep. In addition, it was up to me to have homework done on time and prepare for exams or assignments when they were due. There were times when I neglected these responsibilities, and the consequences were not pleasant. In retrospect, this was good training, as it certainly made my military experience easier. The IBM Corporation was a highly disciplined company. If someone lacked strong organizational skills, he or she quickly learned to remedy the problem if he or she had visions of career longevity.

As I traveled further along the journey of life, being organized assumed a role of greater importance. I learned the value of organizing my plans and goals and how I would be able to achieve and realize them. We have two choices in our lives—we can let things happen and hope for the best outcome, or we can develop a plan and organize what is needed to achieve our objective. This is no easy task, as it requires serious introspection. Some examples would include:

- An assessment of our strengths and lesser strengths
- What career path would we like to pursue
- What kind of education and training would be required
- The importance of material things
- Would marriage and children be a goal
- Geographic location to establish residence
- What would bring us happiness and satisfaction
- Religion, politics, public service as part of lifestyle

This list is without end. It is important to think about who we are and what factors are important for planning our future. This is a fluid exercise and may very well change as we encounter multiple experiences and circumstances on our journey. By organizing our priorities and goals, we develop a road map to reach our ultimate objective. Reality dictates we will encounter obstacles along the way. To put this in perspective, I remember a saying my mother would often recite that she learned from her mother: "People plan—G-d laughs."

It is true we cannot control the future. Life can and does take unusual turns. Situations occur over which we have no control.

We experience both happiness as well as sadness. Some things work out well and some do not. The lesson I learned was introducing and practicing organization in our lives will serve as a rudder on our ship as opposed to being a cork in turbulent waters.

Value Learned: Being organized saves time, reduces confusion, fosters efficiency, and avoids chaos.

PATRIOTISM

Love of our country is an obligation
It should be forthcoming without hesitation

Love of country was instilled in me from my earliest childhood days. Both my maternal grandfather and my father immigrated to the United States very early in life. My grandfather was in his early twenties and my dad was eighteen. Without exception, whenever the family was together, they would express their admiration for America. They came from peasant backgrounds and continuously marveled at the quality of life in the "New World." They were both born in Russia/Lithuania, which was always referenced as "The Old Country." The fact they had opportunities that would never have been afforded them in Europe was the source of boundless appreciation. They continually reinforced the message to me of how fortunate I was to be born in our wonderful country.

I clearly recall the years of World War II and the sacrifices citizens were asked to make in support of the war effort. I never heard one negative word about any inconvenience it might take to support our country. I remember my uncles and older cousins being in the armed services and writing about combat situations. I remember there was never a complaint in our home about rationing, "meatless Tuesdays," no chocolate, sugar, pineapples, new cars, tires, and many other commodities. Periodically at night, we would have to close all the curtains in our home, turn off all the lights, and practice air raid drills. All of these events were viewed by our family as patriotic acts to assist the war effort.

Captain Louis Rappeport

American Military Cemetery, Carthage, Tunisia

Great emphasis was placed on supporting our government and helping our country.

Unknown to me, during the same time period, a little girl named Jody was growing up in Indianapolis, Indiana. She too was being raised with an emphasis on patriotism. However, her experience was far more real and painful than mine. She also had uncles and relatives who served in the military. Her father was so moved by events in Europe that even though he had no obligation due to age and occupation, he enlisted in the army. Captain Louis Rappeport was killed in action April 13, 1943, in North Africa. There could be no greater sacrifice than what her family endured to instill patriotic devotion to our country. Due to this tragic event, this little girl never needed any further education regarding the meaning of patriotism. It was another of the many threads that has become our lifelong bond.

One of the reasons I enrolled in ROTC upon entering the University of Minnesota was to help prepare for military service. I never had any regrets about that decision. Upon graduation in June 1956, I received a commission as an army second lieutenant. Jody and I were married two weeks later, and I reported to Ft. Lee, Virginia, on September 8, 1956, to begin my army career. Ft. Lee was the army quartermaster headquarters. Jody was with me and secured her first teaching position in the Chester County, Virginia, school system.

After completing some six months of basic officer training, I was asked, where did I wish to be assigned on a permanent basis? I was given three choices. I selected Fifth Army HQ, Chicago, Ft. Snelling in Minneapolis, and finally, "just leave me here at Ft. Lee." In true military style, the response was, "We are sending you to an installation in Rochefort, France." I saluted, said, "Yes, sir," and that ended any further discussion or questions. We packed our belongings, set off from Ft. Hamilton, New York, on a World War II troop ship named the USS *Buckner* with our beloved beagle Carmel, and arrived at our French destination on May 1, 1957. I was reminded on a number of occasions that I was doing my

2nd Lieutenant, Herschel Kahn

Cold War medal

"patriotic duty." I must admit, there were times when I started to question the meaning of the word. It proved to be a wonderful learning, maturing, and meaningful experience—one which we will always cherish and one in which many lessons were learned. To "walk the walk," Jody and I embarked on a mission to visit some of our country's most cherished tributes to patriotism. We have toured all the wonderful buildings and monuments in Washington, DC, walked the Arlington Cemetery, visited Ellis Island, Mount Rushmore, and the Liberty Bell in Philadelphia.

I have attended a senate hearing and visited the White House.

I believe that patriotism is an ongoing commitment. We are proud to fly two flags each day at our home, one by the front door, the second overlooking the back landscape. One of my most memorable patriotic experiences occurred when a friend of mine who was a veteran of the Vietnam War asked if I would accompany him to visit the Vietnam Memorial in Washington. He explained that to visit it alone would be too difficult for him. I agreed, and together, we made the trip. While at the wall, I experienced seeing not only my friend, but others as well overcome with emotion, which drove home to me the meaning of patriotism. I have had the honor and privilege of being a board member of the National Museum of Patriotism. This organization is dedicated to promote patriotism throughout our land at every demographic level. Since our inception as a republic, our country has done countless things to make our planet a better place. I am proud to be an American, and I am proud to practice patriotism.

Value Learned: I appreciate being a proud citizen of what I believe to be the greatest country on earth. A country that provides the opportunity to enjoy "Life, Liberty, and the Pursuit of Happiness."

PERSEVERANCE

Don't give up before you reach your goal
Perseverance will overcome the obstacle

At best, I was an average student. I enjoyed the social aspect of school and did not particularly like to study. That combination resulted in a very undistinguished academic record. To compound matters, my older sister was a good student and established an act that was difficult to follow. It was not uncommon in those days to compare siblings' achievements and comment accordingly. This would prompt statements such as "Are you sure you are from the same family?" I was content to maintain my low profile and get by.

All was going well until one very memorable day in May 1949. At that point in my life, I was a fifteen-year-old, typical teen ready to move on in life from the ninth grade at my junior high school to what I thought to be a quantum move to the big leagues otherwise known as high school.

My homeroom teacher asked me to come see her after school one afternoon. She began our conversation with, "Herschel, what are your plans now that you have finished junior high?" I quickly replied that I was looking forward to attending North High School with all of my friends. Her response was quite surprising when she said, "Herschel, you are not high school material and should really consider going to a vocational training school."

I was surprised, and told her that I was not good at vocational skills and barely knew what end of a screwdriver to use. She went on to say that I would not be able to compete with other students at the high school level.

I clearly remember walking home in tears, wondering, Was life over at fifteen? I was both sad and embarrassed.

North High School, Minneapolis, Minnesota

When I walked in the house, my mom asked what was wrong, and I shared with her the entire conversation that had taken place with the teacher. My mom sat down with me at the kitchen table, gave me some milk and cookies, and began her pep talk. She was quite calm and gave me some invaluable advice. She said that I need to have a goal, work hard, never quit, and try my very best to accomplish my goal. I never forgot her advice, which translated to "get your act together, do your best (which you have not been doing), and results will come." She said, "If you really want something and are willing to put in the effort, success will happen." What a wonderful introduction to perseverance.

The story did not end with the kitchen table conversation. I did go on to high school, and after completing my sophomore year, I returned to the junior high and showed my first-year report card to my former teacher. While the grades were not noteworthy, I did pass all the subjects and was promoted to the high school junior level. I also tried out for the track team and was accepted. The teacher looked at what I presented and her comment was, "I'm very surprised, but I would be even more surprised if you make it through the second year." Her lack of encouragement was disappointing, to say the least. The second year, while uneventful, went by quickly, and I now found myself part of the senior class. After graduating, I visited my teacher one more time, proudly showing her my high school diploma.

Her reaction was to ask another question. "I'm surprised. What are you going to do now?" I told her that I was planning to enroll at the University of Minnesota. Her response to that was, "You must be joking!"

When I showed her my acceptance letter a few weeks later, she could not contain herself, and made one final discouraging comment. "Herschel, it's obvious they have lowered their standards." That was the last contact I ever had with her, but the obstacles she put in front of me served to drive me forward to persevere.

As the years have passed, I continually reflect on the challenges that have come my way that through sheer perseverance have been overcome. Obstacles have become challenges. Both in my personal as well as professional life, I have learned that taking no for an answer is not always acceptable. We live in a world of rules, directives, bureaucracy, and some individuals who like to say, "It cannot be done." We cannot overlook the fact that obstacles must be balanced with reality, authority, and common sense. However, perseverance used judiciously (as my family has taught me) can produce positive outcomes together with great personal satisfaction.

DePaul University, Department of Management

MANAGEMENT UPDATE

SCOTT YOUNG, CHAIRMAN
LAUREN RICHERT, EDITOR

May 2015

THE STORY OF A MITZVAH
By Scott Young, Chairman

Herschel Kahn was a DePaul MBA student in the 1970s who went on to a distinguished career with IBM and now runs an HR Consulting Firm in Atlanta. I met with Herschel recently and he told me an interesting story.

He took a Statistics course during his MBA program and none of the eight students could understand the Professor. Seven of the eight students failed, including Herschel. At that time, a failure in any MBA class required immediate dismissal from the program. Feeling that the course was unfair, Herschel requested a meeting with Father Cortelyou, a Vincentian Priest and then a DePaul administrator, to appeal his dismissal. Certainly, Herschel argued, that if seven out of eight students fail, there is something wrong with the Professor and not with the students. Father Cortelyou replied, "I am sorry son, but these are the rules. You are dismissed from the program. God Bless You and I wish you the best in the future."

Herschel walked away, dejected, and as he left the office turned and said, "Father, I am Jewish and do not know much at all about the Catholic religion, however in my religion we are taught that if you see a man that has fallen to his knees, and you stop to help him to his feet that is considered to be a MITZVAH (Hebrew word for a good deed). I don't know if that applies to your faith but I wanted to share that with you." Father Cortelyou stared at Herschel for what seemed like an eternity (probably I minute) and said "Son you are back in the program!"

Herschel went on to tell me, "What an example that was to me of someone having significant authority that could reverse a decision after seeing the logic of another person's view. I have never forgotten that experience or Father Cortelyou."

There are several important points to this story. First, Herschel was absolutely justified in appealing his grade. This was a case of a Professor's failure, not the students'. Not all professors are just, and neither are all lawyers, judges, politicians, accountants, bus drivers, etc. Second, take Father Cortelyou's sense of fairness. Some people might never back away from taking the position that a rule is a rule and there can be no exceptions.

There is a building named after Father Cortelyou on the DePaul campus. He earned that honor. His obituary in the Chicago Tribune included this comment:
"He was very attuned to what was going on around him and was interested in all of that, particularly in the welfare of the students at the university, to whom he had devoted his whole life," said Rev. Ralph Pansza, Father Cortelyou's religious superior at the DePaul Community House for Vincentian fathers and brothers."

His "welfare to students" included the Herschel Kahn reinstatement into the MBA program, and Herschel went on to a very successful managerial career. There are times in every educator's career that they can make a real difference in someone's life and this is a perfect example.

Another example of perseverance that had a fortuitous outcome occurred while pursuing an MBA at DePaul University. I, along with seven other students, was enrolled in a statistics course. English was not the native language of the professor. As a result, it was next to impossible to understand both the lectures and the verbal exams. Seven of the eight students, including myself, failed the course. The academic standards of the university were such that one failure in a graduate course resulted in dismissal from the program.

Given the circumstances contributing to my failing grade, and not looking forward to explaining the outcome to my loving wife, I decided to appeal my case to a senior administrator, Father Cortelyou. His initial reaction was one of understanding, but he was unyielding about any compromise to the academic standards of the graduate school. After my logical argument advancing the fact that seven of eight students failed may have some reflection on the instructor, I went down a theological road. I said that, being Jewish, my faith considered it a blessing or what we termed a "Mitzvah" if we came upon someone who has fallen and helped them rise up. "Father Cortelyou, I don't know what the Catholic faith believes." He looked at me for what seemed an eternity and said, "My son, you are back in the program."

I never forgot that experience; not the value of both perseverance on my part nor the value of compassion on the part of Father Cortelyou. This event was recounted in a DePaul University Management Update in May of 2015.

Value Learned: Never give up, keep trying—additional time and effort may be required to succeed.

PROACTIVITY

Thinking ahead provides a fast start
It is a trait that will set you apart

As a youngster, I was asked on many occasions, "What do you want to be when you grow up?" My answer was always the same: "I don't know." That worked for a while, but then my mom said I should start thinking about what I would like to do. I came up with the usual answers: fireman, policeman, baseball player, and milkman. There were two others that put my mom in a panic mode. They were garbage man and hobo. She could not believe the last two and really quizzed me on those choices. I thought a garbage man had an exciting job as in those days they rode on the outside of the truck through the back alleys and waved to all the neighbors. Our home was within walking distance to a viaduct where the hobos would congregate, awaiting the next freight train. In those days, it was perfectly safe to visit with these individuals and listen to their stories of traveling all over the country in a boxcar. Needless to say, what my mom thought of my selection and her reaction was very clear, forceful, and raised some doubt about the stability of her son. She quickly provided some alternatives such as doctor, lawyer, or concert pianist. Doctors I certainly did not like. I didn't know what a lawyer did, and I never liked the piano as I watched my sister practice for hours on end. In summary, the subject was put on hold until I became a bit older and in her mind much more mature.

School was not my favorite activity, and my scholastic achievement reflected my commitment to studying. As I approached thirteen,

I had to prepare for my bar mitzvah, which required significant effort on my part. At that point my parents left the suggestion mode and became much more direct. They strongly emphasized the importance of preparing for the future. They stressed traits such as thinking ahead, setting goals for oneself, and putting forth the effort to accomplish the goals. They brought to my attention the results of individuals who did not look ahead and had little to show for their years. In their own way, they led by example and demonstrated how they planned ahead be it for family events, business, and financial situations.

Reflecting on my life, there have been multiple decisions that being proactive clearly was a difference maker. That is not to say that looking and planning ahead will always have a positive outcome. However, it minimizes surprises and disappointments. I have selected eight significant examples of being proactive that in retrospect had an immeasurable impact on my journey.

DECISION TO PURSUE A COLLEGE EDUCATION

Like so many high school graduates, getting a job and having money in my pocket had great appeal. However, it became readily apparent that I didn't have any unique skill that qualified me for any rewarding career path. I also observed that most of my relatives that went to college were doing quite well.

The University of Minnesota was just a short streetcar ride away, my dad offered to pay the tuition, and my friends had decided to attend college, so the decision was not difficult. I truly believed making that decision would serve me well.

ENROLLING IN THE ROTC PROGRAM

The year was 1952, and the Korean War was raging. There was talk of drafting young men to support the war effort. I thought if I were required to join the armed forces, it would be to my advantage to be an officer. Also, if by chance I married within the next four years, life as an officer would be more comfortable.

MARRIAGE

I met the love of my life when we were sixteen. Jody and I were meant for one another. We became engaged at the end of our junior year and married two weeks after we graduated in 1956. People thought we were too young, but the decision was without any doubt the absolute best example of being proactive.

APPLYING FOR A POSITION WITH IBM

After my military service ended, I was seeking a position with a well-established company that offered the opportunity to advance on merit, was respected in the marketplace, and had significant growth potential. IBM certainly met all those criteria. That decision was the second best I ever made. The first, without doubt, was marrying Jody.

EARNING AN MBA

In a competitive company such as IBM, I was thinking about what I could do to distinguish myself from my peers. The field of human resources was in its infancy and in my judgment, an MBA in human resource management would open doors when the opportunity presented itself. I graduated from DePaul University with an MBA in June 1970. This decision reinforced my confidence in being proactive.

RETIREMENT

My career with the IBM Corporation was absolutely an incredible experience. I was offered a position in 1959 as mailroom clerk. The facility was the Midwest regional office located in Chicago. I remember being disappointed that my entry-level job would be in the mailroom. I voiced my opinion that I believed having a college degree and being a recently discharged army officer would qualify me for a more responsible assignment. The response to my comment was, "Everyone here starts in the mailroom." I then asked how long would I be in the mailroom. The next response was "IBM is a merit company, and you may never get out of the mailroom." That was the first and last time I discussed career opportunities.

I worked in the mailroom for about three months and then progressed to a clerical position. I had a number of different administrative jobs and in 1962 was promoted to my first management assignment. Over the years, I was fortunate enough to move through the management hierarchy to an executive level. I enjoyed the different challenges and appreciated the opportunities that were afforded to me. My career path was in human resources, an area that was growing, challenging, rewarding, and most interesting.

None of the advancements provided to me would have been possible without the support, dedication, and commitment of my wife Jody. The long working hours, missed family events, and work that was brought home all were met with some choice comments and questions. However, she was understanding and supportive. Many people believed IBM was an acronym for I've Been Moved. That was true in our case as well. Besides Chicago, we also lived twice in Connecticut and once in Cincinnati prior to settling in Atlanta. Jody was by my side through all the hassle. Whatever success came our way, it would not have occurred without her.

In 1991 after thirty-two years with this wonderful company, I started to think about the next phase of life called retirement. I believed that with my experience, the transition to teaching and or consulting would be areas where I could make some significant contributions. I was asked to stay on for one additional year to complete a difficult assignment. Upon completion of that effort, I retired in 1992, having thirty-three years of service.

SHARING EXPERIENCES

After eighty-plus years, the time has come to reflect on my life. I have been blessed and most fortunate to have experienced situations and events too numerous to document. I truly believe that sharing some of these experiences would serve as examples for others to consider.

Too often we are of a mind that someday it would be nice to share some of our experiences with others. However, time passes so rapidly that we either lose our ability to put the plan into action or time has elapsed before we could accomplish our plan.

The work you are reading is one more example of how being proactive can be both satisfying and fulfilling.

Being proactive can mean different things to different people. There are numerous examples of actions a person may take that can be defined as being proactive:

- Keeping an umbrella in your automobile
- Not allowing the fuel gauge to fall below half-full
- Paying taxes before the due date
- Purchasing tickets for an entertainment event in advance for better seat selection
- Adhering to scheduled maintenance for home appliances and automobiles
- Packing for travel prior to day of departure

While all of these qualify as proactive actions, failure to do them can be easily remedied. Ignoring them can lead to frustration and inconvenience, but will have no long-term effect on life's journey. In my opinion, being proactive has a more significant context. I view it as making decisions that can significantly affect your future. Having a goal, planning, and preparing to take advantage of opportunities to achieve our objective is the implementation of being proactive.

Value Learned: It is better to act than react.

Respect for Authority

Respect for authority is something we learn
It is a value someday we too will earn

My dad was a quiet man, but when he spoke, it was quite clear he wanted you to listen. He had great respect for his parents, and he made it quite clear that is what he expected from his children. Being a typical little boy, it was not unusual for me to do some things both in school and outside of school that were not exactly within what my parents deemed to be acceptable behavior.

One day after he learned of an incident that I had been involved in, he summoned me to a one-on-one meeting around our dining room table. Whenever he and I met in that environment, it usually was not the most pleasant encounter.

The meeting began with him asking, "Herschel, do you know what due process means?" I thought for a moment and said, "No I never heard of it, and have no idea what it means." He then proceeded to tell me that the United States of America is the greatest and most wonderful country in the world. One of the reasons is that our country believes in and practices due process. He then compared the United States to Russia, his birthplace, in the days of the czar. He said that due process did not exist there and was never practiced. At that point, he had my interest, but he still had not explained the meaning of the phrase. I was becoming impatient and asked again, "What is this thing called due process?"

He then began to explain and define the statement. "Herschel, due process allows both sides of a disagreement, argument, or dispute to be heard." He further talked about there being two sides to every story. "America believes that it is fair and proper that both parties be given the opportunity to explain their respective positions.

My dad's entry card into the US

Now, Herschel, I have some good and some bad news for you. The bad news is that due process does not apply in the house."

My dad had the utmost respect for three demographic groups.

1. Parents
2. Teachers
3. Elders

There was no question that this was instilled in him by his parents.

After reinforcing his vision upon me he described in great detail what this meant for me.

He went on to say that in the event he received a complaint from any member of the above described groups, the only thing he and I would discuss is the punishment. No version or explanation put forth by me would be acceptable. It was made crystal clear, and there was no further conversation to be had.

He went on to explain that everyone has to understand and more importantly respect authority.

He also explained that as one becomes older, parents, teachers, and elders might not be directly involved in your life. However, while in this house, that rule stands. He firmly told me that it was my job to ensure that he never received any complaint from my mom, a teacher or an elder—the only exception being if my older sister had a complaint.

These were not idle words and he did enforce them on occasion. One example occurred when as a teenager, I was told to be in the house no later than 11:00 p.m. I did not adhere to that directive and came home much later than the appointed hour. The next morning, Dad was not pleased. He asked me to go with him outside to our backyard. The yard was enclosed by a short, white picket fence. Dad said that since I seemed to enjoy being out late, he would give me an opportunity to repeat my adventure. However, this time, I would have to stay outside within the confines of that fence for twenty-four hours. My mom could bring me food, but I could not come back in the house for twenty-four hours. He ended the conversation by saying, "For your sake, I hope it doesn't rain." After about two hours, the sky opened and a deluge began. I could hear my mom in a loud voice asking my dad to let me in saying, "He will catch cold!" My dad did not relent and exactly twenty-four hours later, I was allowed to come inside. In today's world the action taken by my dad would probably put him trouble with the law, and I would be sent to foster care. In retrospect, I'm happy I grew up in the time period I did.

My father, Sam Kahn

Many people for whatever reason don't understand or have significant difficulty in respecting authority.

Life is much easier and one can avoid significant problems if this is understood at an early age. Respecting authority does not mean complete and total capitulation and blindly following all directives.

As one continues on life's journey, we need to learn how to balance our own individual thoughts and beliefs with orders given by others in positions of authority. There is a time for commentary and there is a time to remain silent. There is a pathway to challenge authority in a diplomatic manner. To summarize, it is my belief that this becomes a function of maturity.

An analogy I would use is that as children, we are at the back of the line of life. Ahead of us are parents, grandparents, teachers, and managers. As time goes by, the people ahead leave the line. Sad as it may be, they pass on, retire, or for other reasons go in other directions. As these events occur, we move up in line and we find that now we are in the positions of authority and there are more people behind us in line than when our journey began.

While authority must be respected and used prudently, it should not and cannot be followed blindly. Obviously if one is directed to commit an act he or she knows is clearly wrong, an exception to this rule is in order. Judgment which requires some intellectual processing must prevail. It also would be most helpful to understand the organization chart under which you are operating.

Value Learned: Understand the chain of command. Use judgment but always be respectful.

Retirement

Retirement is a sought-after goal
Use what you learned and assume a new role

As a youngster, when I had to wake and get ready for school, I remember how nice it would be to sleep late. In college, I remember how nice it would be to spend the day doing whatever I desired as opposed to listening to a boring lecture. As an adult, I remember how good it would be to avoid the hassle of commuting either by car or train. The thought of retirement seemed so very distant—why waste time dreaming about something so far away? In addition, my vision of retirement was of very old people just sitting around and telling stories about the "good old days."

One key lesson about retirement resulted from a conversation I had with my father. He and my uncle owned and operated a furniture store that specialized in both new and used furniture. They began their business as Kahn Brothers Complete Home Furnishings in 1910. Their business model was selling anything to furnish a home. The inventory ranged from dishes to desks and clocks to carpet. By the time I was a teenager, they were no longer interested in growing the business but were content to use it as a place to visit with people that would stop to browse. Their attitude was if someone purchased something that would be fine, and if not, that too would be all right. One day when discussing the business with my dad, I asked the question, "Why don't you just sell the business and retire?" He answered with two questions to me: "Why would I retire and what would I do?" Before I could respond, he continued with his explanation. His message was that one must always have something to do and someplace to go. "This store gives me a chance to meet people, help them, and learn new things." He summarized his message with, "There is food for your stomach and there is food for your brain. Both are key to life. My message to you, my son, is don't ever retire."

When his brother died in a tragic accident in 1965, Dad walked out of his store for the final time. He could not bring himself to be there without his brother. The sudden death of his brother was a debilitating loss to my father. He never recovered from that event and spent his last years at home with my mother. He lived an additional nine years and passed away at the age of ninety-three. He had very little education but was a great teacher.

It was my good fortune to work for a wonderful company. IBM provided many challenges as well as opportunities. Each assignment gave me the chance to learn new things, meet new people, and apply the experience gained to future endeavors. I was fortunate to have worked with many wonderful people. Their support, loyalty, and guidance made it possible to advance from my first position in the mailroom to a human resource director level position. At the age of fifty-eight, after thirty-three years, I retired on July 31, 1992. It was time to start a new chapter in life.

I remembered what my dad had taught me about retirement and decided that I would do something else. Jody was fine with the idea but did deliver a clear message in her own direct way. "If you want to retire, fine, but don't think you can just hang out around the house and try to manage me!"

The transition from a fast-paced business environment to one far less demanding was not difficult. I had heard that many people found it quite stressful and described it as coming to a sudden stop after traveling at a high rate of speed. This was not the case with me. I had done some planning and it was just a matter of implementing the plan. Jody and I had wanted to do some traveling, and she as usual did a great job with that activity.

I thought it would be interesting and self-fulfilling to do some lecturing at the college level. This fell into place when I was given an opportunity by Georgia State University to be an adjunct professor and executive in residence in the W. T. Beebe Institute of Personnel and Employment Relations.

The teaching experience led to some independent consulting opportunities, and I developed a small but interesting client base. The next activity that I believed would be challenging involved volunteer work. I thought it would be both meaningful and fun to offer my professional experience to assist an organization in need of human resource and general business experience. The opportunity arose when I volunteered to help the International Executive Service Corp. (IESC). This is an economic development not-for-profit organization headquartered in Washington, DC. The IESC Russian experience during the winter of 1995 served a dual purpose. It reinforced my belief there is life after your primary career has concluded. Secondly, there is great self-satisfaction in realizing people can contribute in a positive manner, utilizing the experience they have accrued. It proved to be both a learning and teaching experience for me. I still maintain contact with the gentleman I helped and have watched his progress from a startup to a mature, thriving, and very profitable entity.

The consulting background led to yet another enjoyable and intellectually stimulating experience. I have received and accepted invitations to join the board of directors of several different companies. These opportunities have provided an insight into different enterprises and meet very interesting people while helping with the challenges they encounter.

There also has been plenty of time to travel, develop hobbies, visit friends and relatives, and just enjoy all that life has to offer. Retirement has been fun, stimulating, and nothing to fear.

The lesson learned was plan for it, do it, and enjoy it. As my father taught me, make sure you have something to do and some-place to go! He would say, "Remember, son, feed your brain."

Value Learned: Retirement is transitioning into a new phase of life. It provides you an opportunity to share experience, learn something new, and enjoy both.

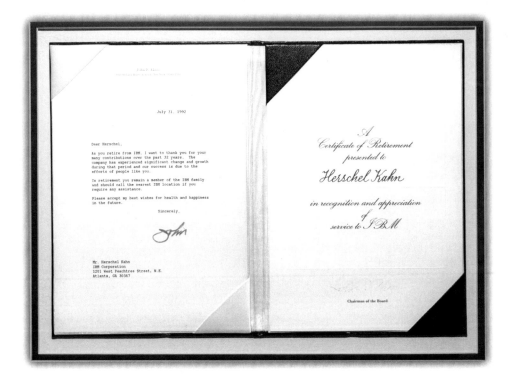

Thirty-two years with IBM

Stress

Stress is troublesome and can wear you down
Make a decision to remove that frown

Dealing with stress is one of the most difficult challenges anyone has to face. It enters our lives continually and if not controlled can have disastrous impact. Stress comes in many different sizes and shapes. Examples may have their genesis in issues such as:

- Family
- Finance
- Career
- Health
- Aging
- Geopolitical events
- Interpersonal relationships
- Meeting schedules
- Time management
- Expectations of others

These are but a few representative samples that can be problematic. Stress is not governed by any boundaries, whether they be age, gender, economics, position, notoriety, education, or other societal metrics.

Over the years, I have had the privilege of interacting with and observing many people in all walks of life. One example would

include senior executives having significant management responsibilities that maintain an air of complete composure. At one
point, I asked one individual how he could appear to be so calm
given all the responsibilities and issues he faced on a daily basis.
His response was quite simple and direct. He asked how many
employees reported to me. My response was none. He then added
that he had two thousand reporting to him. He continued, "I don't
worry because they know they have to fulfill their responsibilities.
My suggestion to you, young man, is work hard so someday you
also will have many people under your management."

I have seen pilots, physicians, retail assistants, and teachers
under stressful conditions that appeared calm and under control.
I have also interacted with executives, sales personnel, and contractors
who mirrored the stress they were under. At one point I had the
responsibility of assisting individuals in transition between jobs. The
biggest challenge I faced was not to prepare clients for seeking a
new position, but rather to help them relieve the stress they were
under. I have seen them in all types of situations and conditions.

- Not sharing their situation with their family. I have
  seen individuals go off dressed for work each morning
  as if nothing has occurred.
- Financial concerns. "How will I pay my obligations?"
- Social stigma. "What will my friends and neighbors
  think about me?"
- Loss of self-confidence. "There must be something
  wrong about me."
- Self-pity. "Why me, Lord? I came to work every day,
  worked hard, and performed well."

While I did not realize it at the time, I was learning from them
the lesson of managing stress. Some did very well and accomplished
their objective with minimal strain. Others had quite the opposite
result. In my family, there were examples of behavior that were

on both extremes of the spectrum. The same was true in my military and professional careers. Friends, business associates, faculty, and people in general cope in different ways. I conclude that we all manage this phenomenon in a personal style.

Over the years after encountering a number of stressful situations, I decided to construct my own personal model that helped me immeasurably in moving through stressful situations. I named this model the "Two Bucket Theory."

"TWO BUCKET THEORY"

The initial premise is that into everyone's life problems will arise. I have yet to meet the person that has not experienced any problem on life's journey. Visualize a cloud that contains problems, some of which are designated for us to deal with. The cloud releases the problems and now they become our challenge to resolve. The range of severity is infinite.

Examples:

- You were planning a picnic and woke up to a thunderstorm.
- You forgot to do an errand your spouse assigned to you.
- You experienced a car problem on the way to an appointment.
- You arrive at the airport and learn your flight has been cancelled.
- The checkbook balance is zero and some critical payments are due.
- You learn that a loved one has received a terminal diagnosis.
- You are not happy with your job.
- You have an early appointment and oversleep.
- Your home has been burglarized.
- The stock market plummets.
- The "wrong" candidate prevailed in the election.

The list is endless.

The next step in the process is to visualize two buckets. One bucket is labeled "Things I am able to change." The second bucket is labeled "Things I am unable to change."

The visualization continues. The problems that are outside of your control go into bucket one. You cannot do anything about them. The problems that you can do something about go into bucket two.

The loss of a loved one or a terminal diagnosis is devastating. We can turn to prayer or get another diagnosis but most likely the outcome will not change. That repository is bucket two.

When a flight is cancelled and no other flight is available, we have no alternative other than wait for the next flight. The other issues we do have the ability to eliminate or greatly reduce the level of stress go into bucket one.

It is critical to understand that actions have reactions. All things in life have a price. Placing issues in bucket one comes with a price. The question to be answered: Is the action worth the price?

For example, if one is not happy with his or her job, he or she can resign and get a different one. The price may result in less income, thereby impacting the quality of life you have been enjoying. You may be dining on filet mignon today and hamburger tomorrow. If income does not support expenses, one may either cut expenses or get a second job to increase income. Both choices have a price.

Geopolitical events are a great concern. Thinking about somewhere outside of our country there exist others that have the capability of destroying not only our country but civilization as we know it can be not only stressful but depressing. We can voice our concern and support appropriate causes, but in the final analysis, as individuals we cannot change the situation. Unfortunately, that issue must also reside in bucket two.

The lesson learned is if you can change something and are willing to pay the price, then do it. If you choose not to do something, then accept things for what they are and go on with your journey.

Worrying and stressing usually lead to additional and bigger problems. The end result is more stress.

Value Learned: If you encounter a problem that you can do something about and are willing to "pay the price" to remedy the situation, do it. If you are unwilling or unable to "pay the price," live with the issue and don't stress over it. If you encounter a problem that is beyond any of your control, accept it for what it is and recognize no worry or stress on your part will remedy the problem. You will naturally express emotion, but understand the issue is outside of your ability to change the outcome.

Taking Responsibility

Taking responsibility may be difficult to do
However, it speaks volumes about you

"It wasn't my fault," "the dog ate my homework," "I ran out of time," and "the traffic was terrible." These are but a few of an endless number of excuses we have all heard at one time or another. Unforeseen events do occur and things beyond our control can certainly happen. However, as we journey through life, we learn the road traveled is much smoother if we accept the responsibilities required to arrive at our destination.

When I reflect on my childhood, I recall multiple situations that portrayed accepting responsibility. I did not realize at the time the role my parents played in teaching the acceptance of responsibility. My dad immigrated to the United States from Russia as a teenager, arriving January 1, 1900. He worked hard and as he accumulated the funds, he brought both his parents and his siblings to the New World. He made sure they were all provided for, and only after each was settled did he marry while nearing the age of fifty. My mom got a job after graduating high school and contributed to her family for their support. They both clearly exemplified the meaning of taking responsibility.

Our household was clearly one of division of labor. My mom accepted all the household functions. My dad accepted all the financial responsibilities. My sister and I were expected to do our homework, help with chores, and get along with each other. There were several additional requirements relating to behavior that were expected of me.

As I think back, the household model we had worked well. I had to get to breakfast on time, leave for school on time, and be home on time. Homework was to be done in a timely manner and complaints about my behavior had dire results.

As the years passed, this training paid dividends as it made transitioning to adulthood easier. In college, it was clear what was required of me to graduate on schedule. It became an intelligence test to experience the resulting penalties being irresponsible brought.

The next phase of learning about responsibility came when marriage appeared on the horizon. It was made abundantly clear to me that once marriage took place, you were on your own. Asking for financial assistance was not an option. The same message was also a component of my wife's training. This was actually a blessing in that neither one of us felt the need to seek family financial assistance. Once married, we set off on our own and accepted all the responsibility that goes with that life-changing event. When purchasing our first home, I did ask my mother-in-law for a loan. It was a non-interest-bearing loan and was expected to be repaid, which it was.

After our marriage, the next phase of learning about responsibility began. I entered the service and was sent to France to operate a military commissary. I was accountable for government assets valued at approximately $3 million.

My wife, Jody, taught school and also understood responsibility, as she had to comply with all the teaching requirements expected of her.

The next responsibility lesson was without a doubt the most important of all. Jody and I began a family of our own. Raising four children, providing for their health and welfare, being role models, and teaching the values that would serve them through their lifetimes is a privilege that brings with it monumental responsibility. Even as the torch of adulthood has been passed to the next generation, we still feel responsible for assisting when called upon. At times, the line between assistance and dependence can become somewhat blurred.

Raising my family

I quickly learned taking responsibility in my professional life was a key ingredient to success. The IBM Corporation was a fantastic organization to be part of. People had performance plans that articulated what was expected of them. If an employee performed well, recognition was forthcoming. Often recognition of a job well done would provide a promotional opportunity. Acceptance of the new opportunity came with accepting additional responsibility.

I learned that performing well was viewed as a condition of employment. In the event one had ambitions to maximize his or her potential, there would be a need to demonstrate some distinguishing characteristic. Observing others who achieved successful careers was a lesson well learned. One fundamental characteristic that I found to be common with career progression was being creative and accepting additional responsibility. This was especially

161

valuable if the additional responsibility was outside of your assigned tasks. As I reflect on my IBM career as well as my consulting experience after retirement, accepting additional responsibility has been a most satisfying experience.

It is not easy to accept responsibility. On any given day, the media is replete with example after example of individuals not accepting responsibility for their action or inaction. It appears convenient to shift responsibility to others for situations that we should have or could have addressed. Mistakes are part of life—they happen. Errors in judgment and poor decisions happen. The person that has the fortitude to stand tall and accept responsibility earns and deserves the respect of others. The person who deals with the situations life offers and accepts the risks and rewards should be viewed as special.

Time Management

Time is perishable and doesn't stand still
Managing it is a sought-after skill

"Herschel, time to wake up!" It was the 6:30 a.m. clarion call from my mother Monday through Friday. There was no second call or any other substitute for a snooze alarm. Little did I realize at the time my mom was teaching me the value of time management. I was expected to be at the breakfast table within fifteen minutes. Then off to school I went. My punctuality record at school received the same scrutiny, as did my overall report card. Tardiness was simply unacceptable.

Activities in our home generally adhered to designated timeframes. Meals were served at specific times. The evening news on the radio had an assigned time. There was a time to study and a time for play. The key theme was to be on time. This level of discipline has served me well throughout my life.

As the years have passed, I have gained an appreciation that time is a most interesting commodity. We are given a finite amount of it each day. We cannot buy more, trade, or sell what we have been given. It is highly perishable and cannot be put into a savings account. The age-old quote of "use it or lose it" is very appropriate in describing its usage.

I have concluded that there is a direct correlation between accomplishments and time management. Everyone is granted 168 hours per week. How we utilize those hours is the key to realizing whether or not we can attain our goal, meet our objective, or discharge our responsibilities.

I recall a number of people that reinforced the value of time management I learned as a child.

My parents: They insured things were done on time, appointments kept, and being late was perceived to be a character flaw.

My wife: I am absolutely amazed how Jody could manage the house, raise four children, teach school, do some volunteer work, plan trips, and find time to create and craft over a hundred custom-designed quilts she presented as gifts.

Executives: Having interacted with some very successful executives of high-profile enterprises and observing how they could multitask, lead, by example, handle stress, and exceed assigned goals while maintaining their composure has been a unique experience.

Friends: One friend in particular has a family, travels, and maintains a professional career. He decided to enter the Iron Man competition. This triathlon event consists of a 2.4-mile swim, a 112-mile bike ride, and concludes with a 26.2-mile run over a seventeen-hour timeframe. Competing requires hours of training each week. He was committed to his objective and achieved world-class recognition. This as a result of his dedication to his goal and his ability to manage twenty-five hours per week to train while simultaneously addressing his primary responsibilities.

The list is without end when I realize that almost everyone has a responsibility to adhere to a schedule. The challenge is how one allocates time to accomplish all that is expected of him or her.

I have learned there are some specific requirements necessary to successfully manage time:

- Develop a plan
- Organize
- Prioritize
- Resist distractions
- Do not procrastinate
- Do not allow obstacles to discourage you
- Anticipate problems

- Delegate and inspect
- Realize not every task will be enjoyable
- Self-discipline is critical

These are but ten of many components of successful time management. When I feel overwhelmed and think there aren't enough hours in the day, I review the factors noted above and regain my composure.

During our lifetime, we think and dream of many things. There comes a time when a call to action happens. This can be self-motivated or we can receive varying strengths of advice and counsel to provide motivation. The ability to manage our time properly is crucial if we expect to achieve our objectives.

Our goals are unlimited and may be simple or difficult. We may strive to improve our financial situation, achieve a promotion, lose weight, take the trip of a lifetime, pursue higher education, changing careers, adapting to new technology, volunteering to helping others or improve our interpersonal skills, or try to solve what seems to be an insurmountable problem. Whatever our goal, it will require managing time.

"Herschel, time to wake up!" was a great lesson. The introduction to the word "time" at such an early age has had a profound impact on how I perceive this most valuable gift we receive each day we awake.

Value Learned: Time is our most precious commodity. Its value dissipates with each passing second.

TRAVEL

The world is large with much to do
Travel is interesting and educational too

The world really isn't flat. I can attest to that by firsthand experience. Growing up, my world consisted of a five square mile area in North Minneapolis. My relatives, friends, schools, and playgrounds were all located within that limited area. On rare occasions, my dad would drive outside of that zone, but that was only for a reason that had to be something special. On occasion, our family would drive to Little Falls or Detroit Lakes, both within two hundred miles of our home. Once in a while, we even ventured twenty-five miles across the state line into Hudson, Wisconsin, for a special ice cream treat. When I was sixteen, I joined a United Synagogue youth group and did attend youth conventions in different cities. These included Chicago, Des Moines, Omaha, and Kansas City. I was seventeen when I took my first trip by air. The first time I saw a mountain occurred when I attended ROTC summer camp at Ft. Carson, Colorado, between my junior and senior year at the University of Minnesota. At that point in life, I was perfectly content to stay within my comfort zone relatively near my home.

Then came marriage and the world was no longer flat. There is no doubt in my mind that somewhere in Jody's heritage resided the genes of Marco Polo, Christopher Columbus, or Amerigo Vespucci. This lady was born to travel. What a great teacher she has been. Her mother often said, "Why should there be a place that I haven't visited?" My dear wife has taken that to a new level.

The lesson she taught me was the world is filled with fascinating places and interesting people. Her goal was to meet as many people and see as many places as possible. One can read about far-off places. We can also study and see pictures of people in their native habitat practicing components of their culture and observing their religious beliefs. However, to actually witness these things and meet people from around the globe serves to transform thoughts into reality.

The journey began with our honeymoon drive from Chicago to Acapulco in 1956, and continues to this day. Over the years, we have visited all fifty states, most of the national parks, and every major city in our country. We have visited over eighty countries and sailed many seas and oceans. In addition, we lived in France and Russia. Prior to our marriage, Jody lived in Israel for a year. That was her introduction to understanding what travel had to offer. In a feeble attempt at humor, I sometimes suggest we sell our home and rent an apartment within walking distance to the airport. My dear wife does not appreciate my sarcasm.

Our first cruise

Great Wall of China

A question that is commonly asked is, "What was your favorite place or city to visit?" My answer is always the same. Every place is different and has something to offer. If I had to prioritize travel experiences, at the top of my list would be an African safari. The reason being that you can visualize the Eiffel Tower, London Bridge, pyramids, Sydney Opera House, Taj Mahal, beaches of Rio, the Western Wall in Jerusalem, the Great Wall of China, the crowded streets of Tokyo, the Leaning Tower of Pisa, the Roman Coliseum, Vatican, Kremlin—and on and on. These are stationary historical places and objects that await our viewing. They have a place in history. However, to drive along a trail at daybreak not knowing what may be beyond the next curve and perhaps see ten giraffes walking slowly in the morning mist, a herd of elephants all following their leader in one direction and protecting their young by keeping them inside the herd, a female lion protecting her cubs while feeding them, or a leopard lounging in a tree awaiting nightfall is an experience of a lifetime. I compare the safari experience to opening presents on our birthday. You never know what may be inside the box—each is a surprise.

Continental Divide

Travel is not the easiest activity. Schedules to adhere to, delays, cancelations, long and bumpy flights, rough seas, unpredictable weather, adventurous diets, and a variety of personalities to deal with all contribute to some degree of stress. However, the benefits far outweigh these inconveniences. Our fondest memories not only involve the sights to be seen, but the personal relationships that resulted from all the trips. We have friends literally across the globe with whom we maintain contact as a result of meeting on a trip years ago.

One important lesson that I consider to be self-taught is not to compare our quality of life at home to that which we experience when traveling. At times there is a tendency to long for the comforts of home—air conditioning, hot water, central heat, a paved highway, television, endless supplies, and varieties of food or spacious living accommodations, to name just a few. What I have learned over time is to psychologically place the comforts of home in a storage container in a closet and do not think about them when traveling. There is no point in longing for something that is not within reach. Upon returning home, take these comforts out of the container and enjoy and appreciate them.

Jody and I have been fortunate to have traveled the globe. Most activities have both positive and negative aspects. Travel is no exception. It can be tiring, frustrating, and sometimes dangerous. However, from my perspective it has been one of life's most exciting and rewarding experiences. It has been of tremendous educational value. Things, wildlife, and places that one would see only in a book come to life and become reality. The understanding and actually living in different cultures is mind-expanding and provides an understanding of how individuals behave differently. The social benefits can and do lead to life-long relationships. We maintain friendships with people we met over fifty years ago. Travel provides an opportunity to leave our everyday stress and routine to relax and enjoy what a different lifestyle has to offer. It serves as a nonmedical prescription to improve both physical and mental health.

I have friends that are very happy to remain close to home. I can appreciate and understand their view. Everyone has their personal comfort zone and that is to be respected. It is no different than individuals having different tastes when it involves food, music, clothes, colors, or hobbies. From my perspective, I'm delighted to have been introduced to the world of travel. The experience has served to enrich my life. It has been a lesson that has benefited me greatly and one that continues to pay dividends with every trip. Thanks to Marco Polo, Christopher Columbus, Amerigo Vespucci, and my wife Jody, I have learned the world really isn't flat.

I consider it to be a most pleasant, educational, interesting, and healthy addiction.

Value Learned: See as much of the world as you can while you can. It is a treasure awaiting discovery.

India

TRUST

Worthwhile relationships are built on trust
To realize your goal, it is a must

We have all heard many quotes that describe this value. They include "in G-d we trust," "trust but verify," and the simplest of all, "trust me." In all cases, they translate to the expectation of taking a leap of faith. The common denominator in trust is the reliance that what is stated is true, what is written is factual, and what is promised will be realized. It takes time and results to earn trust. However, it can be lost in minutes by a single act—rarely, if ever, to be regained.

In my youth, I recall numerous situations and conversations between my dad and grandfather describing both good and bad examples of trust. Dad had numerous examples of people to whom he extended credit to that always repaid their debts as well as those that elected to not pay. My grandfather had similar commercial experiences but also had examples that were pointed to the character and moral fiber of people. He talked about a person that publicly voiced how much money he was contributing to a synagogue-building fund. When it came time to write a check, the individual had a memory lapse and could not recall his public pledge. Both my grandfather and father were quite adamant about the value of someone's word. While they may not have been articulate, I came to appreciate their belief that trust is the cornerstone of any relationship. That was long before Jody ever responded to the question about trust in marriage. No wonder they loved her. One of the supreme compliments they could offer about someone was, "They can be trusted." At the other end of the spectrum was a description appropriate for someone deserving capital punishment. My dad was quite liberal in extending credit to his customers. Credit reports and scores were not in vogue during the period he was in business. He relied on his judgment and intuition. In the event he erred, it would only happen with a client one time. Word of mouth tarnished the offender's reputation beyond repair. Checks were accepted without supporting identification. Many times a document would be signed without benefit of legal counsel. Society was far less litigious. A person's word prevailed.

The world of commerce has undergone immense change over the years. This has given rise to countless new industries and technologies—all of which have as one of many objectives to counteract the diminution of trust exacerbated by activities such as credit card fraud and identity theft.

Trust is not confined to commercial events. It permeates all facets of our lives. Each day, the media highlights examples of the erosion of this value. We have witnessed individuals in elected office, the judiciary, high-profile athletes, clergy, academics, and military all having compromised the trust bestowed upon them.

I have learned that trust cannot be bought, given, or inherited. It must be earned over time. On occasion when an unfortunate situation occurs, we hear the phrase, "They were too trusting." At the opposite end of the spectrum is the declaration, "If that person said something, you can take it to the bank." I recall numerous examples whereby my parents honored commitments made when a reasonable excuse would have relieved them of the responsibility. One of my dad's favorite quotes was, "Without your word, you have nothing."

On the occasion of our fiftieth wedding anniversary, Jody and I were asked an interesting question: "If you could choose one word to define your long marriage, what would it be?" My answer was "Compromise." Jody's answer was "Trust." To me, that was the ultimate compliment.

Jody and me, 1955

Everyone at one time or another is given multiple opportunities to exhibit trust. We may be privy to confidential material, conversations, financial transactions, or other events all not to be disclosed. How we accept this responsibility defines our ability to be trustworthy. This value must be learned it is not generic. Just as we learn of situations that highlight lack of trust, we also become aware of situations whereby trust has prevailed.

I have had the fortune of being surrounded by a circle of family, friends, and business associates that viewed trust as a way of life without compromise. I was employed by a company that could accept and tolerate various deficiencies, but was unyielding when it involved a violation of trust.

In retrospect, this highly prized value has been learned from multiple people and organizations. It is a characteristic that is under constant challenge as society evolves. However, it is a value that has and must continue to prevail. Perhaps our founding fathers should have added a few additional words to those on our coins and currency—"In G-d we trust. All others, pay cash."

Value Learned: Your word is your most valuable asset.

TRUTHFULNESS

Being truthful may cause some pain
In the end respect you will gain

"Tell the truth" was drilled into me from my earliest memory. Leading the charge was my grandfather. I vividly remember how he spoke of people that did not tell the truth. He could accept most of their actions. However, his view of lying was nonnegotiable. My dad was not far behind with his view of someone that was not truthful. I was taught that mistakes happen. At times, people will make poor decisions and poor choices. When those situations occur, one must tell the truth, take responsibility, and accept the consequences of their actions. Telling a lie to escape responsibility was unacceptable.

My mother took a more logical approach. Her message was that one lie will lead to another. At some point, one will not remember one false version from another and the entire story you are trying to tell will collapse. The main theme she kept emphasizing was if you have to tell a lie, you most likely did something wrong.

From my perspective, truthfulness seems to be in general decline. Continually, the media will call attention to people in all walks of life choosing to be less than truthful regarding their involvement in specific events. No profession is immune to such behavior. Unfortunately, it permeates politics, athletics, commerce, theology, public, and private sectors as well as the general population.

As a youngster, I certainly participated in my share of situations that were not something to be proud of—whether it involved not doing homework, talking back to an adult, stealing apples, misbehaving in Hebrew school, being late for dinner, missing curfew, losing things, and on and on. As each event came to the attention of my parents the drill was the same. "Why did you do that?" I would then give reasons that I knew were untrue. They ranged as follows: the homework wasn't due until tomorrow, I did not talk back to the adult, the apples I took had fallen from the tree and I just picked them up, the Hebrew teacher was picking on me, I forgot to wind my watch and it stopped. The next question was, "Think carefully and tell me once more—is your story true or are you telling a lie?" This was then accompanied by a warning that lying will only make things worse. That usually closed the case.

As an adult, I would on occasion still experience some embarrassing situations but came up with more plausible reasons to explain my behavior. I presented them as reasons but in reality they were excuses. These would include: I mailed the check last week, there was a traffic problem that delayed me, when I woke up this morning I didn't feel well but I'm better now, and I didn't forget, I just misunderstood. Some would describe these statements as white lies. In the spirit of truthfulness, a lie is a lie.

One lesson I learned from my mother: when confronted by someone wanting an explanation about something you were alleged to have done, you have just two choices—either yes, I did that, or no, I did not do that. Anything else is not telling the truth. If you answer "I can't remember" or "I don't know," that counts as a lie.

After sixty years of marriage, I have learned another answer that has prevented a potential storm. When Jody purchases something and asks my opinion of her choice, rather than express a negative answer which would be truthful, I have developed a much more diplomatic reply which has avoided any conflict. The answer that has served me well is, "If you like it, that is all that matters to me. I just want you to be happy."

Truth is one of the most important and basic pillars that form the foundation upon which our reputation rests. If people are unable to take our word, whatever attributes we may have are greatly diminished. As human beings, we will err, avoid responsibility, exercise poor judgment, and make poor decisions. We can recover from all of these setbacks. When we lose the trust and confidence of others due to not being truthful, the damage is severe and lasting. The lesson I have learned is while truthfulness can hurt, maintaining our good name will make the pain go away.

Value Learned: Telling the truth is not always easy to do, but it says volumes about you.

WEALTH

With wealth one can acquire things of value
Don't let the pursuit of it consume you

Our family was neither rich nor poor. I would describe my dad as a fiscal conservative. If he purchased an item, it would be of high quality and payment would be made in cash. He never understood why people incurred debt. This philosophy was in direct conflict with a core segment of his business. He owned a new-and-used furniture store. A significant segment of his customer base purchased furniture on a credit basis. He kept a ledger for each customer and they would pay their account on a weekly or monthly basis. He never charged any interest, as he believed his profit alone was sufficient. It was an interesting business model, which was not uncommon in the early 1900s.

The subject of money was rarely discussed in our household. Dad paid cash for our home in 1939. He bought a new car in 1941 and drove it until 1956. He was of a mind to buy a vehicle new, drive it until it stopped, and then purchase another new one. Fortunately, the car he bought was one of the last ones manufactured prior to World War II. All the necessities needed for a quality lifestyle were provided. There was ample money for education, charity and running the household. Things beyond necessities were considered frivolous. These would include routine maintenance, vacations, entertainment, or dining out. My mother paid the bills, but there always seemed to be enough money to sustain our quality of life.

My dad did teach me the value of a dollar and how to use money wisely. My first job was selling newspapers on a corner stand in downtown Minneapolis. At that time a newspaper was three cents, and many people would give me a nickel and say, "Keep the change, kid." I would return home with a dollar or two in pennies and Dad would show me how to put them in penny wrappers. He would take me to the bank and exchange them for currency and taught me how to save for something special I may want to buy.

A great lesson I learned came at the expense of my older sister Harriet. She was given an allowance to go to a movie downtown. On one occasion she had one dime left for streetcar fare home. She elected to use that dime to purchase a movie magazine. Since that was her last dime she called home to ask my dad to pick her up and take her home. His reply was a resounding "NO!" He told her to figure out herself how to get home. When she did arrive the lesson continued when he reinforced the value of saving and budgeting. It wasn't until years later that I realized he wasn't being mean but in his own way was teaching money needs to be properly managed.

When Jody and I purchased our first home, both Mom and Dad came to visit.

One of my dad's first questions to me was, "What did you pay for this house?"

When I told him, his next question was, "Where did you get that much money?"

I explained that the bank owns the house and we have a mortgage. He was very disappointed in what I did, but after some discussion understood that times did change.

Over the years, I have come to realize that money is a means to an end. It is not the end. Money is merely a commodity used to buy things. It has a value that is relative to other things. For example, if a person ran out of fuel while driving across the desert would he or she rather have a hundred-dollar bill or a five-gallon container of gasoline? My parents stressed that money can make a person comfortable, but it cannot bring happiness. To the contrary, it can also bring problems.

My grandfather would repeat over and over, "A poor person can be a wealthy person if they are happy, while a rich person can be poor if they are sad." He went on to impart a valuable lesson to me. If you live a good life, an honest life, and help others, you will be thought of and remembered as a good man. He continued by saying your reputation is more important than your bank account. Obviously he was not ignoring the necessity of having the means to provide for family, but in his own way he was making a greater point.

While one metric of wealth is our net worth, there are other measurements as well. I have come to realize the value of the lesson taught. Wealth is comprised of far more than money. The money we amass and leave behind will be redistributed. The realization that we are happy as a result of what we have done is far more valuable. It sustains us while alive and appreciates long after we are gone. That is true wealth.

Value Learned: Material things are but one spoke on the wheel of life. Who you are, what you have done, and what you leave behind form the entire wheel.

Work Ethic

A strong work ethic is a great plus
It does speak volumes about us

The fact that people routinely worked long hours was part of our family culture. My dad would be up each morning ready to leave the house the same time I left for school. My mom would wake early every morning to insure a hot breakfast was ready and everyone was prepared to begin their day. I remember evenings when my parents took me to visit my grandparents and my grandfather was not ready for dinner because he had some unfinished work to do. This theme extended to almost every family member.

Thinking back where this behavior originated, I concluded it began with the lifestyle they experienced while children in Europe. Survival required long hours with little compensation. My father arrived in the United States as a teenager. He had no family, friends, education, or funds. Long hours and hard work became a way of life. This was the norm at the beginning of the twentieth century. That generation understood the effort necessary to succeed.

The lesson of "work hard and you shall succeed" was not just theoretical in our household. It was applied in a practical manner. I vividly remember a conversation with my dad when I was about ten. At that time movies were twelve cents, an ice cream cone was eight cents, and a streetcar ride was ten cents. I received an allowance of one dollar per week. For that dollar I was required to do some household chores. It did and still does snow quite heavily during a Minnesota winter. Dad thought it would be a good idea if I earned some money by shoveling snow at the house next door. I could earn a dollar for the effort and would be able to have some extra money to spend. I wasn't too excited about the idea, but he explained why it made sense. The point he made over and over was if you want something, you have to work for it.

The next opportunity arrived when I was twelve and got a job selling newspapers at a newsstand during my summer vacation. That job required four hours every afternoon. There were days when I would rather be doing something else but my dad made sure I understood work was not optional. As a teenager, I would ride my bike to a local golf course and wait my turn to be hired as a caddy. Some afternoons were quite hot and the golf bags seemed heavier as I got closer and closer to the eighteenth green. I was beginning to understand not only the value of a dollar, but the effort it took to earn one. More importantly, it became clear that a strong work ethic and success were linked. Maturity brought with it a deeper understanding of the relationship between work ethic and success. While success may very well be accompanied by financial gain, it also has another dimension. The self-satisfaction one experiences upon realizing the work ethic he or she put forth to accomplish a goal often surpasses the material reward. Financial success is but one event that is attributed to a strong work ethic. There are countless others. For example:

- Academic accomplishments
- Athletic accomplishments
- A beautiful landscape
- Learning to play an instrument
- Creating a custom-designed quilt
- Excelling at a hobby
- Community service
- Household projects

The early introduction to work ethic by my family served me well in my professional career. Working for IBM was a privilege that I will forever appreciate. The good news about working for that organization was it offered limitless opportunity. The other side of the equation was it required an incredible amount of time and commitment.

My initial introduction to this way of life occurred with my first administrative assignment. One day I made the mistake of asking my manager what were the office hours. His answer was short and direct: "In the morning I will bring you a file folder containing the work I expect to be completed by the end of the day. When the folder is empty your workday is over. Do you have any other questions?"

I am forever indebted to Jody for her patience, tolerance, and understanding. The late dinners, times having to take care of the children alone, travel, phone calls, vacations missed, or being rescheduled are but a few examples of what her work ethic entailed. Without her support and understanding my work ethic would have been irrelevant.

I was taught that everything in life has a price. If you strive for excellence one must understand work ethic is part of the price to pay. When we see or hear about a gold medal, Academy Award, Nobel Prize, Pulitzer Award, championship trophy, civic, or leadership recognition, we can only imagine the time, effort, and dedication that made the recognition possible. Work ethic is not limited to high-profile events or people. It is a fundamental characteristic that is necessary to maximize our potential.

We have heard comments attributing success to luck, being at the right place at the right time, "it's all about who you know," "they had a lot of help," or "I could have done that given a chance." Whatever goal we set, the recipe for success will require a key ingredient called "strong work ethic."

Value Learned: The road to success is paved with a strong work ethic.

FINALE

While I have tried, and for the most part succeeded in, carrying out the values I have learned, a self-assessment brings me back to reality. It would be disingenuous to say that I practiced every value all the time. There have been occasions where with forethought I elected not to implement the values learned. This is proof positive that human behavior is not always predictable. Fortunately, these behavioral lapses have been outnumbered by those that demonstrated what I was taught.

Life is a journey along a path. We know when and where it begins, but when and where we reach our ultimate destination is forever unknown. Another oddity is the travelers are going in only one direction. We do not see anyone coming back. It is strictly enforced as a one-way artery. The trip is filled with innumerable emotions. Joy, sadness, excitement, fulfillment, love, loneliness, disappointment, and anger are but a few examples.

Along the way, we encounter many experiences. We travel through storms, and also enjoy beautiful days. We meet the entire spectrum of both people and animals. Some are docile, friendly, and helpful. Others may be unfriendly, predatory, and devious. At times the path ahead is straight and free of obstacles. There also are occasions the road may have hills and valleys that must be negotiated. We may come to forks in the road that require decision making. There are situations when we are alone as well as times we are accompanied. The terrain we traverse can appear rock solid, or it may actually be covered in quicksand. We may receive directions, and then again, there will be periods we will be without guidance and decisions are ours alone. It is at that point you as the traveler need to apply the values you have learned to achieve a conclusion that will stand the test of time.

It has been my intention to articulate the genesis of the core values by which I have lived. I have tried to bring these values to life by sharing with you personal experiences which formed their foundation. The values were taught by a long list of people in many venues during my life's voyage—starting with my parents and continuing with my grandfather, other relatives, teachers, clergy, friends, business associates, and of course my wife. Collectively, they have proven to be an incredible faculty.

The values I have learned are analogous to lessons we have all learned in school with two significant exceptions. First, I didn't understand at the time how I would ever use the value being taught. Secondly, the test to determine if I understood the material occurred years after it was taught, not at the conclusion of the grading period. The values have served to make the journey interesting, exciting, productive, and rewarding. Hopefully they will prove to be beneficial to those yet to reach my mile marker.

Make it your responsibility to develop your own personal set of values. Utilize and live by your values to not only guide you through life, but to leave as role models for all who will follow in your footsteps.

ABOUT THE AUTHOR

As an octogenarian, Mr. Kahn enjoys reflecting on his life experiences as well as the values learned throughout his life. His experience base includes sixty years of marriage, raising a family, and thirty-plus years of working in corporate America. He and his wife, Jody, have traveled the world, and take pride in having visited over eighty countries. Adding to that lengthy list, Mr. Kahn and his wife traveled to the Arctic in the summer of 2016.

Beyond family life, his twenty years of retirement have been devoted to serving various causes including the military, consulting, and teaching.

Mr. Kahn lives with his wife, Jody, and their family in Marietta, Georgia.

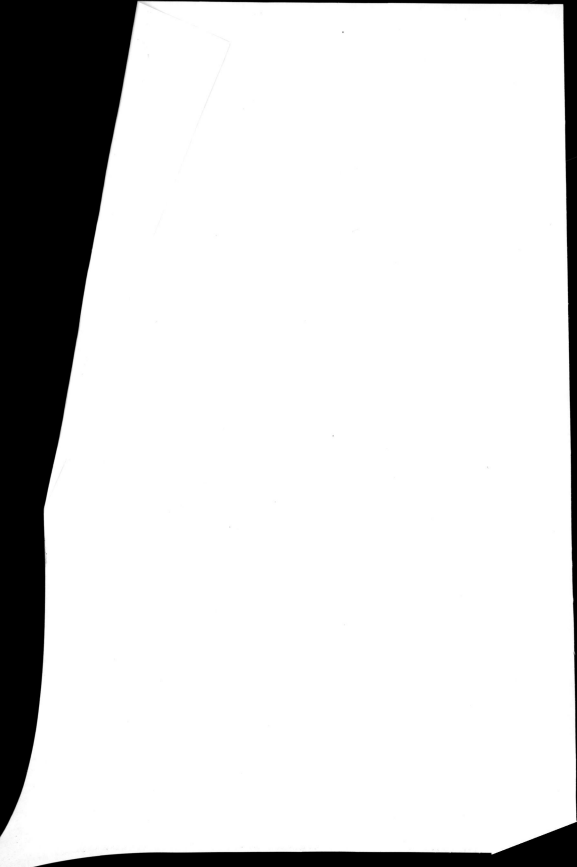